Mac OSX Mavericks Speedy Refe...
Copyright © 2014 by Bluewater Publishing
LLC

All rights reserved. No part of this book may
be reproduced in any form or by any electronic
or mechanical means, including information
storage and retrieval systems, without written
permission from the author, except in the case
of a reviewer, who may quote brief passages
embodied in critical articles or in a review.
Trademarked names appear throughout this
book. Rather than use a trademark symbol
with every occurrence of a trademarked name,
names are used in an editorial fashion, with no
intention of infringement of the respective
owner's trademark.
The information in this book is distributed on
an "as is" basis, without warranty. Although
every precaution has been taken in the
preparation of this work, neither the author
nor the publisher shall have any liability to any
person or entity with respect to any loss or
damage caused or alleged to be caused directly
or indirectly by the information contained in
this book.

# TABLE OF CONTENTS

## Chapter 1 – Your Desktop

## Chapter 2 – Finder

## Chapter 3 – Keyboard Shortcuts

## Chapter 4 – Function Keys

## Chapter 5 – System Preferences Tips

# Chapter 1 – Your Desktop

When you startup your Mac, you will see your desktop:

- At the top of the screen you will see a menu bar. On the far left there is an Apple icon. You can find two important items here, *system preferences* and *About this Mac.* System preferences is where you set things like the background image used on your display, preferred sound input and other items of interest. About this Mac gives you basic information about your computer such as memory.

- To the right of the Apple you will see a text item that changes depending on what you are doing. It tells you what app or application currently has the focus.

- The *Finder* is the file manager for the Mac. It's where you will find folders and documents on your computer.

- The bottom of the window is called the Dock. It has a set of icons on it which act as shortcuts that will open an application. Just move your mouse pointer over an icon and left click your mouse once to open.

- The icons displayed on each dock will in general be different, but you're going to see a few standard items. This includes the Finder icon which lets you switch back to Finder if you have other apps open, the *Launchpad* which provides access to all the apps stored on your computer, and on the far right you will see the trashcan,

where deleted items reside until you decide to
permanently delete them.

If you click on the Apple icon in the upper left on the menu
bar, you will see this drop down menu open:

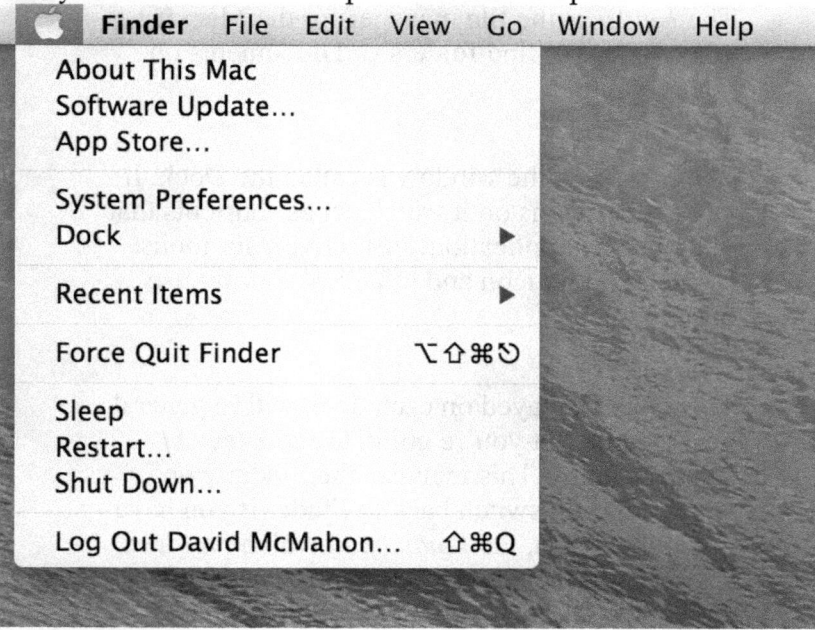

## About this Mac

Clicking About this Mac opens a dialog box with processor, memory and other information about your Mac:

## System Preferences

When you click on System Preferences this screen will pop up:

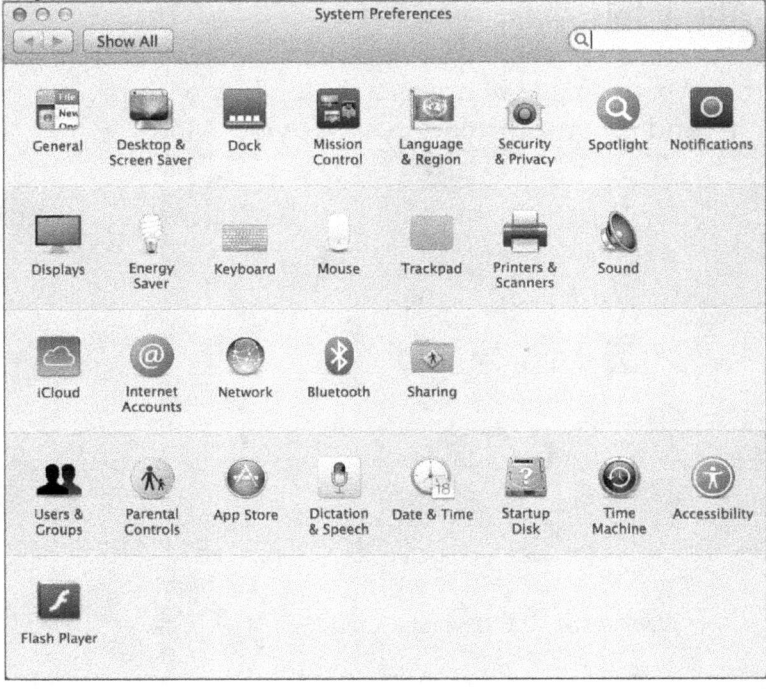

This can be thought of as the "control center" for your Mac. For example, you can set up a printer by clicking on Printers & Scanners, or select your wallpaper from Desktop & Screen Saver.

## Right Menu Bar

Now let's turn our attention to some other menu items you will notice, in the upper right hand corner of your Mac. Specific items may differ a little bit, but most users will see, moving from right to left:

- Messages – displays mail messages *if you are using the Mail app.*
- Spotlight – allows you to search your Mac, for example for an image file.
- Date and Time. Click to select digital or analog display, and to set preferences if necessary.
- Battery indicator (if using a Macbook)
- Speaker Volume – click the icon to open a slider control to turn volume up or down.
- Wifi – click for setup or to join a network
- Bluetooth
- Time Capsule – for backing up your Mac.

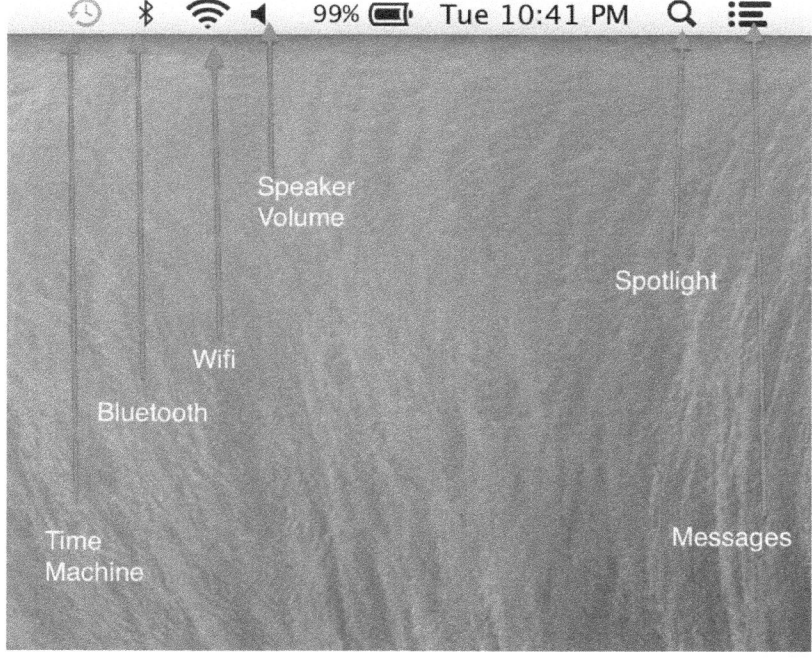

The Notification Center on the right will display app alerts and messages.

## To Open an App

To open a software application, these days called simply an "app", you have a couple of ways to do it.

- Click the Finder icon on your dock.
- Click on *Applications* on the left pane of the finder window that opens.
- Find the app you want to open. You can click once on it to select it.
- Double click to open.

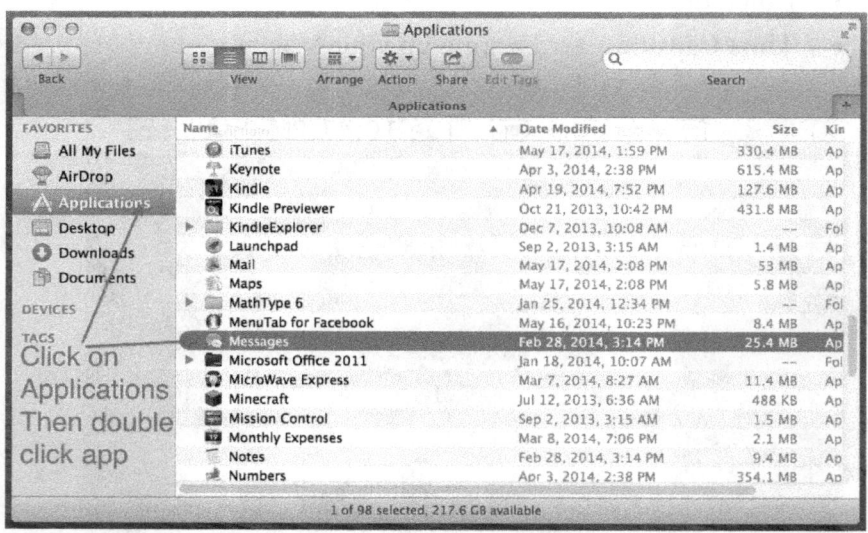

Alternatively, find your launch pad icon on the doc:

Click on it once with your left mouse button. This will open a paged screen showing icons of the apps installed on your Mac. If you are an iPhone or iPad user, this screen is analogous to your device, and you can swipe through the pages.

- If you have a trackpad, you can swipe through the pages using two fingers.
- Alternatively, click the left mouse button and swipe with one finger.
- Or, using the keyboard, press ←⌘< to page left (left arrow + command + less than key) or → ⌘> to page right (right arrow + command + greater than key)
- Left click anywhere on the screen to return to the desktop.
- Click once on an app's icon to open it.

Your launch pad will look something like this when open:

Pressing your escape key will also close launch pad.

## Closing an Application

If you have an application to close it, go to the application's name on the menu bar and click on it. For example, using Microsoft Word you would see this menu:

At the bottom you can click *Quit Word* to close the application. Any application that has the focus - can be closed using the keyboard combination command + Q:

⌘Q

There is a third way to quit an application. When you open an app, it's icon will appear on the dock. If you left click and *hold* a menu will open above the icon, which includes a Quit option:

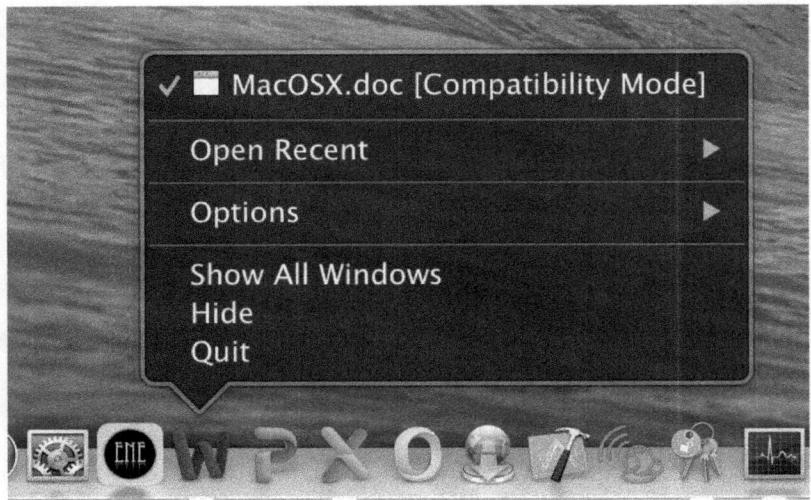

Left click on Quit once to close the app.

## Trashcan Notes

If you left click and hold on the trashcan you will see a menu popup. You can either open the trashcan to view its contents, or select empty to permanently delete the files currently in the trashcan.
If your trashcan has items in it, it will appear as though full of paper.

To delete files:

- Open a Finder window
- Navigate to the folder containing files you want to delete
- Click on a file with your left mouse button to select it.
- To select multiple files, after selecting the first one, press control + command while left clicking file names with your mouse.

- Click the *Action* button at the top of the finder window
- Click *Move to Trash.*

Alternatively, you can hold down your left mouse button and manually drag the files you want to delete to the trash can. When you see the word "Trash" pop up when your mouse pointer is over the trash can area, release the mouse button. If you release when "Trash" is not displayed the files will be dropped onto the desktop.

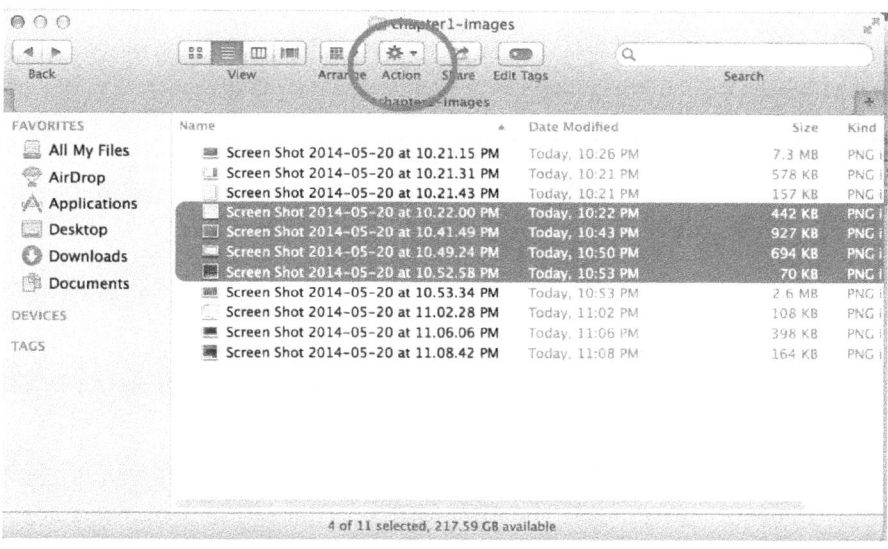

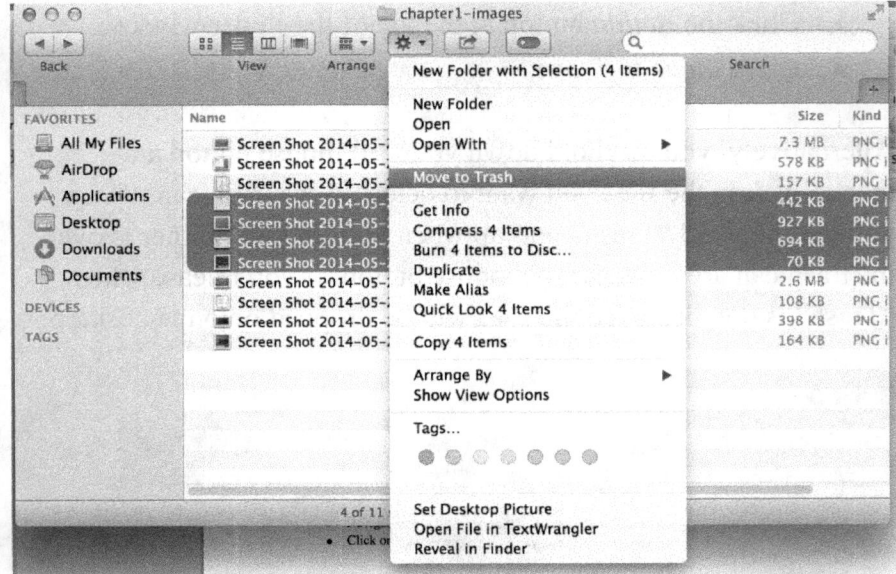

# Chapter 2 – Finder

Finder is an application that lets you manage the folders and files on your hard drive. Finder is always open, but you can make it the active application at any time by clicking on the Finder icon found on your dock:

This will open a window like this one:

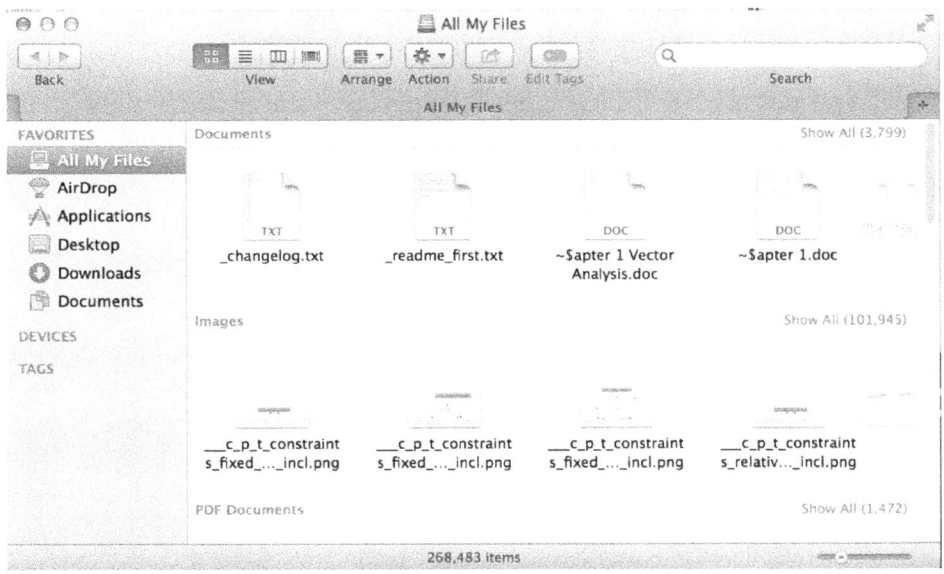

The first item to note is the list on the left side of the window. Items here include:

- Downloads – folder where your downloads from the internet are typically placed.

- Applications – folder that contains the software applications like word processor and spreadsheet program installed on your computer.

- Desktop – the desktop is just another folder. You can save frequently used files to the desktop for easier access.

- Documents – the Documents folder is the central folder for most users. You can store your word processing documents, images, and so on here.

- Airdrop – a way to share files wirelessly between two different Macs. More on that later.

If you put a USB drive or DVD into your computer, it might show up on the left panel as well.

Navigation through folders is standard and similar to what Windows users are familiar with.

- Left click on a folder to select it.

- Double click to open.

- Use arrows in upper left for navigation similar to using a web browser.

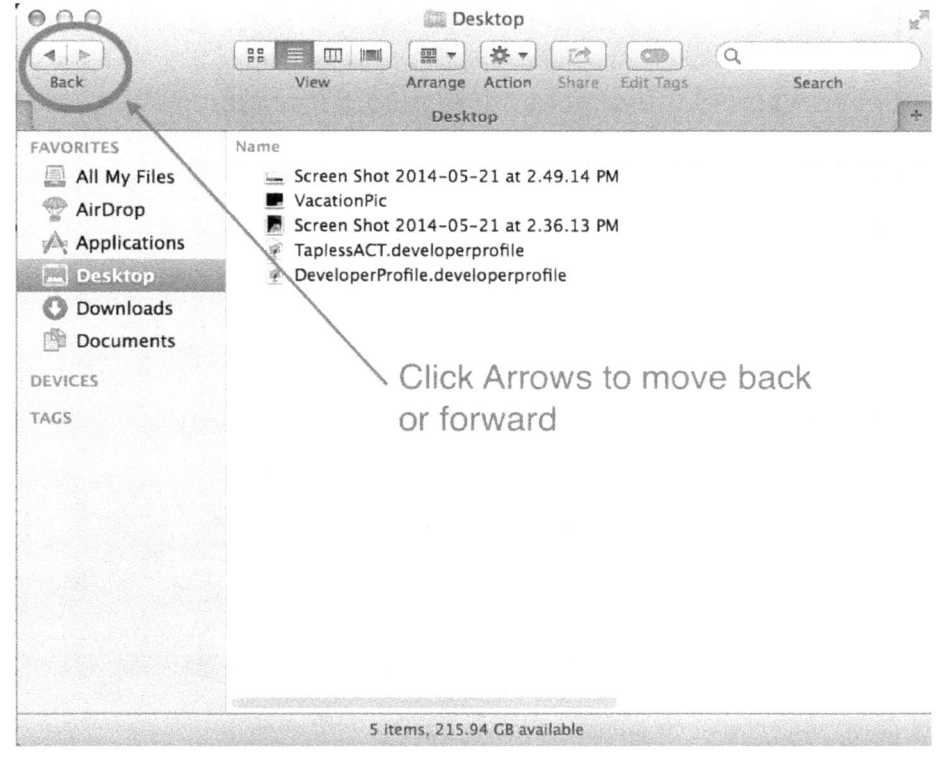

## Moving a File

Suppose I want to move a file from one folder to another. One way to do it is to open two folder windows and drag the file from the source folder into the destination window. In this example, I will move a file from the desktop into a folder where it will be permanently stored.

First we begin by opening two finder windows. The window on the left is the desktop and the window on the right is the destination folder.

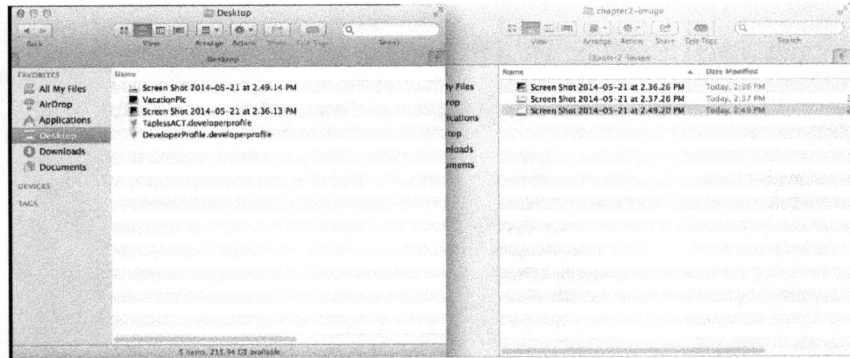

Click on the file you want to move (left click on it once).

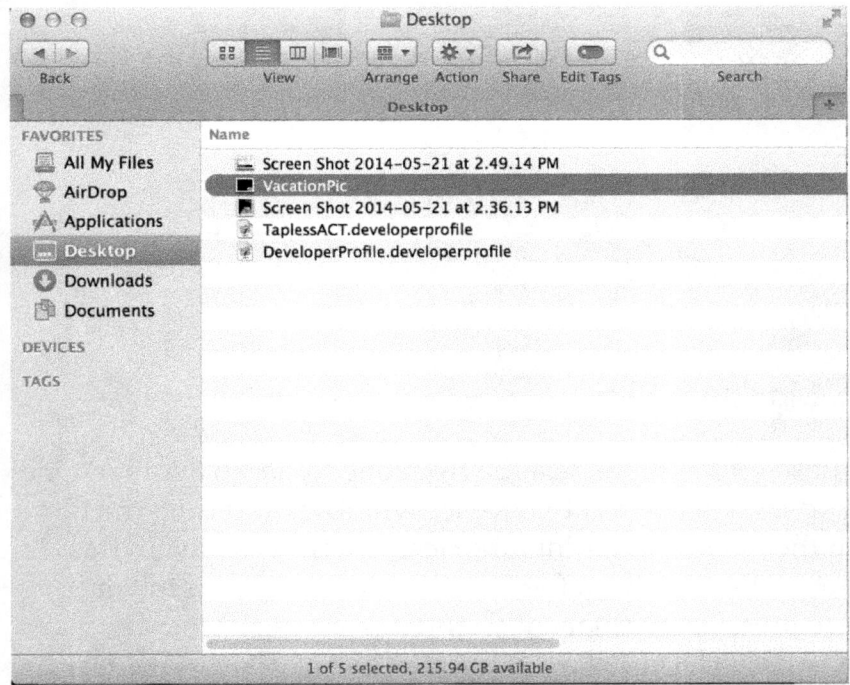

Now hold the left mouse button down to drag it into your destination folder.

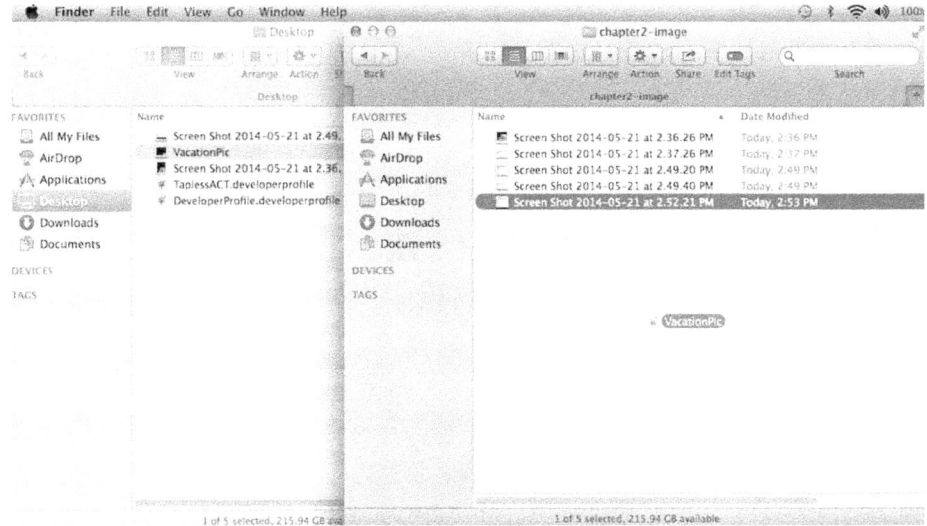

When your mouse is over any portion of the destination folder, release the mouse button and drop the file.

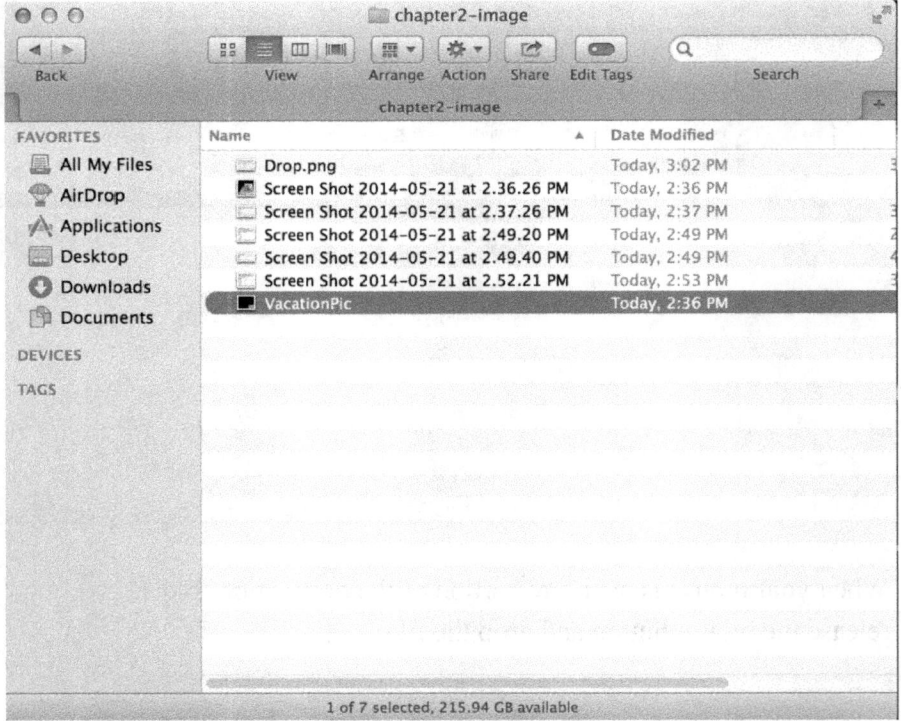

## Opening a File

To open a file, use one of these three methods:

- Locate it in a Finder window. Double click it. This will open the file with the default software program or app for that file type. For example, if you double click on a png or jpg image, it will open the file in Preview.

- Left click on the file to select it. Click on the File menu for Finder in the upper left. Select Open or Open With. See image below for selecting a different program (GIMP) to open a PNG image.

- Select the File you want to open. Click the Action button at the top of your Finder Window, and select either Open or Open With.

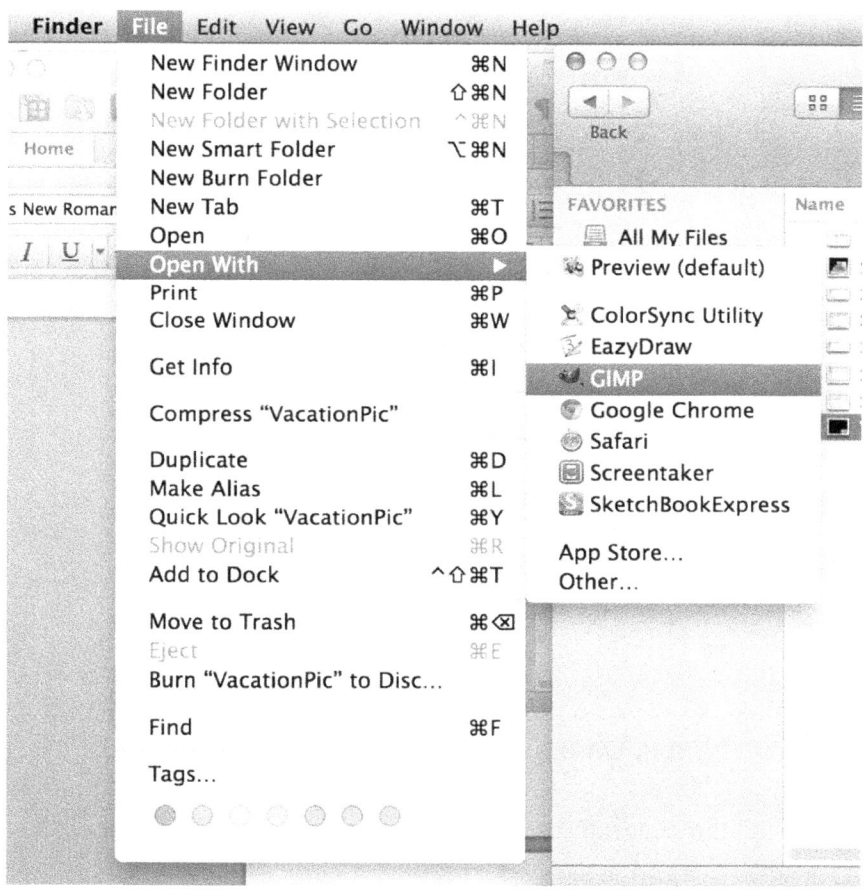

The File pull down menu for Finder, which allows you to open a file using a non-default program by selecting *Open With*. Alternatively, as shown below, access the Action button in your Finder window.

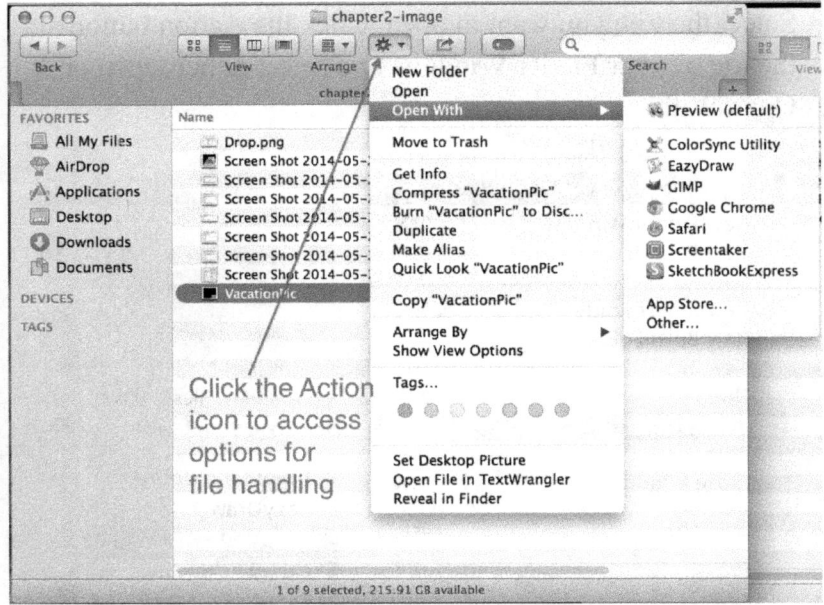

Click the Action icon to access options for file handling

## Sorting Files

Finder allows you to sort files in several different ways. You can sort by Name, Date Created, or arrange by file type. To sort:

- Find the heading for the sort order you want. For example, open a finder window and look for *Date Modified.*
- Simply click on the header to sort the files. Click again and it will sort in reverse order.

## Tagging Files

Tagging files allows you to label files for importance or urgency. Tags are displayed as colored circles next to the file name. The meaning of the colors or tags is entirely up to you. You can tag files or folders. To tag a file:

- Click on the file or folder you want to tag
- Click either the Action button on the finder window toolbar or select the File menu in the upper left when you have Finder as the active application.
- Click on the color you want to tag the file with.

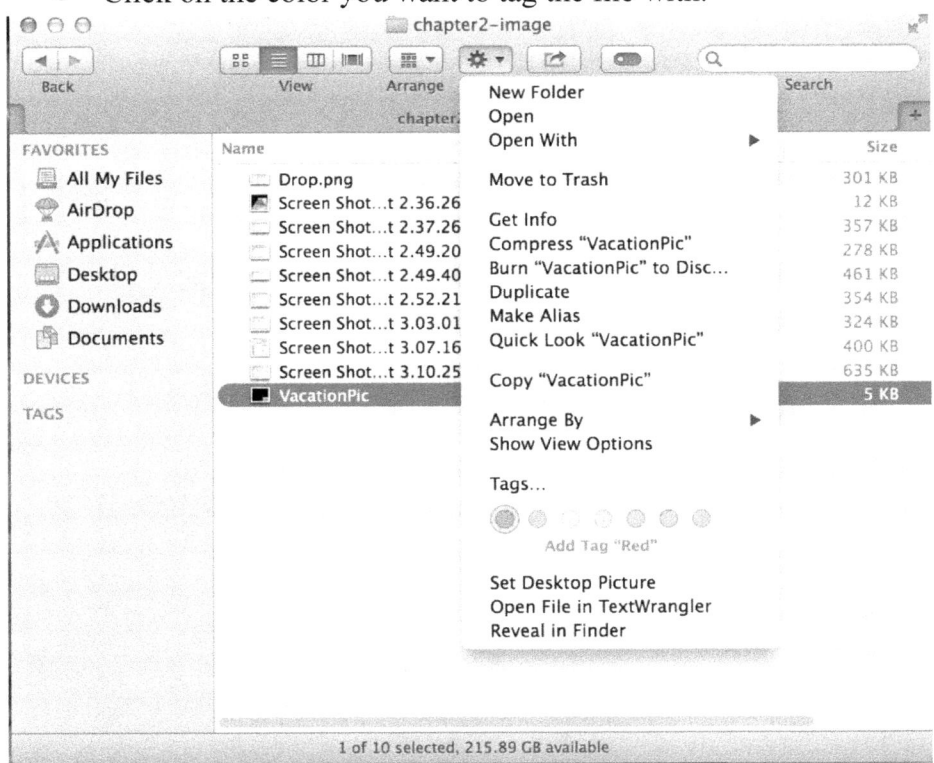

Selecting a tag for our file. For example, click on the red tag. After tagging, the file will appear in the finder window as shown here:

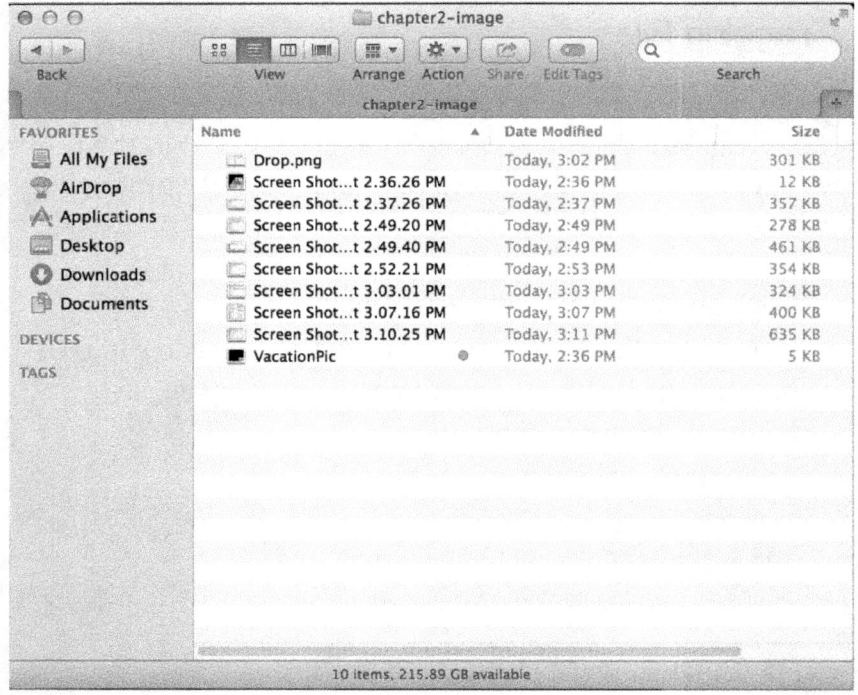

When viewing files from within an application, the tagged file will clearly stand out:

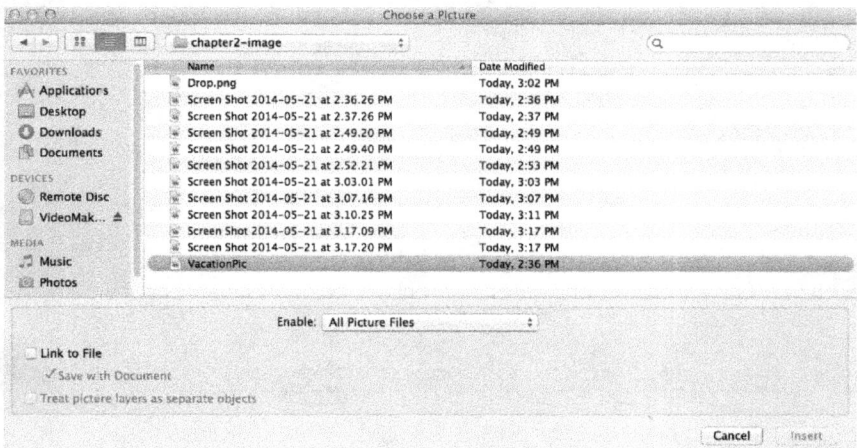

## The Right Mouse Click

Another way to see menu options for a file or object is to right click. The ability to right click may not be available for all users. If right clicking does not work on your computer, press the control key and then click the mouse (control+click). This will open the Finder window for the file:

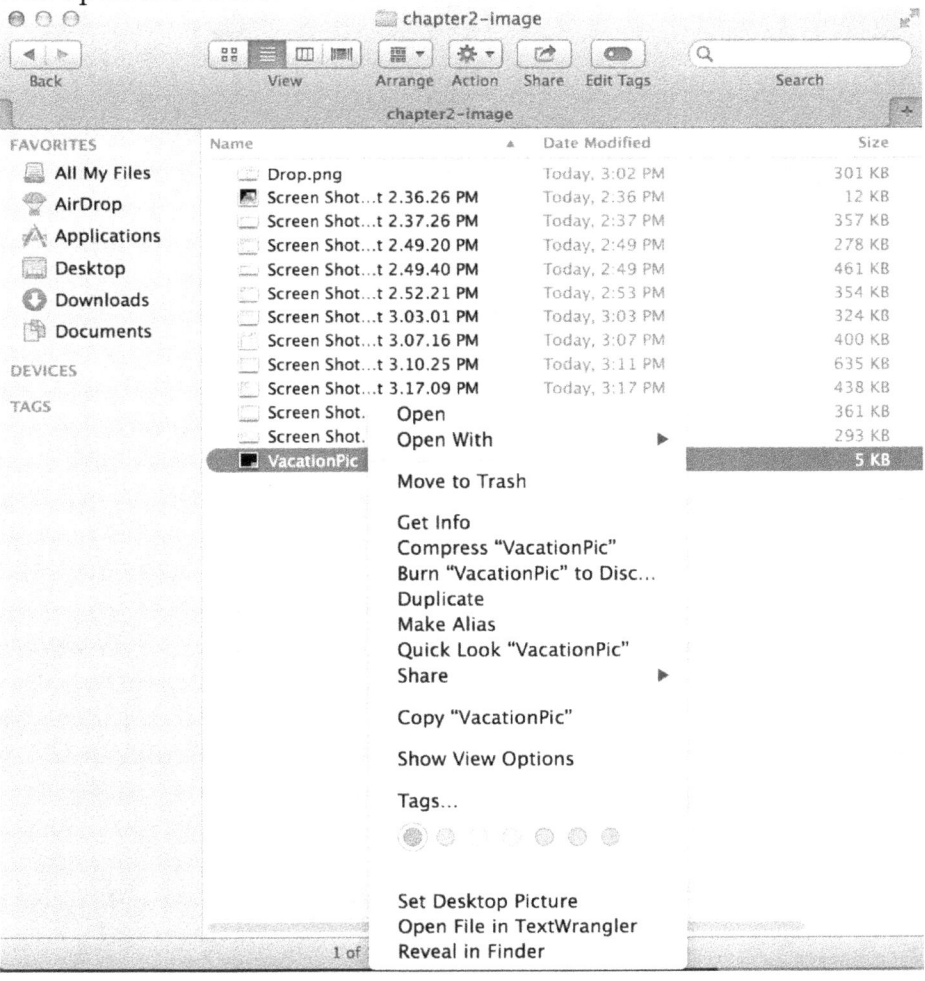

## The Go Menu

The Finder has a menu item called *Go*. This is found in the top menu bar of your computer when you are using Finder. It gives you quick access to important folders like Downloads and Applications. You can also open recently used folders as shown here.

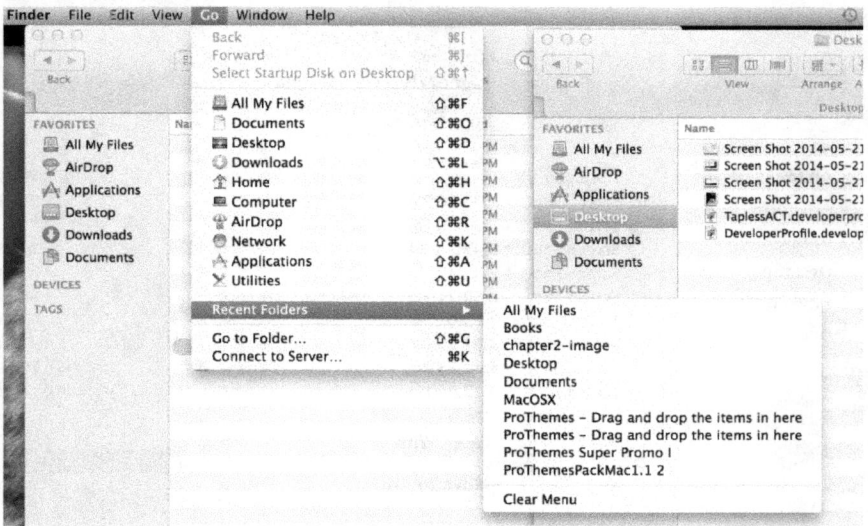

## The Home Folder

Every user on a given Mac has a home folder indicated by their user name. To access your home folder:
- Open a Finder window
- Press ⌘+**shift**+**H**

## Open, Close or Minimize a Window

In the upper left corner of a window you will see three icons:

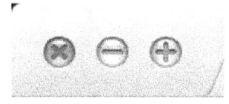

Moving from left to right:

- Close a window (red) – will close the open window. This can be a finder window, a document inside an application, or even close the application itself.
- Minimize (yellow) – moves the application to your dock. You can reactivate the application by clicking on the dock icon. The application is still running while minimized.
- Maximize (green) – gives the application maximum or full screen size.

## File Stacks

A shortcut to your downloads folder called a *stack* can be found on the dock. If you click on it, you will see the most recent files saved to the folder open in a fan-like pattern:

Clicking on one of the icons that opens here will open the file or folder. You can add your own stacks to the dock.

- Open a Finder window.
- Select the folder you want to function as a stack.
- Drag to the dock and release.

Caution: Be careful not to drag the folder into the trashcan on the dock when doing this.

## Recent Items

If you click on the Apple icon in the upper left, you can access the Recent Items menu which displays recently opened applications. Simply click to reopen.

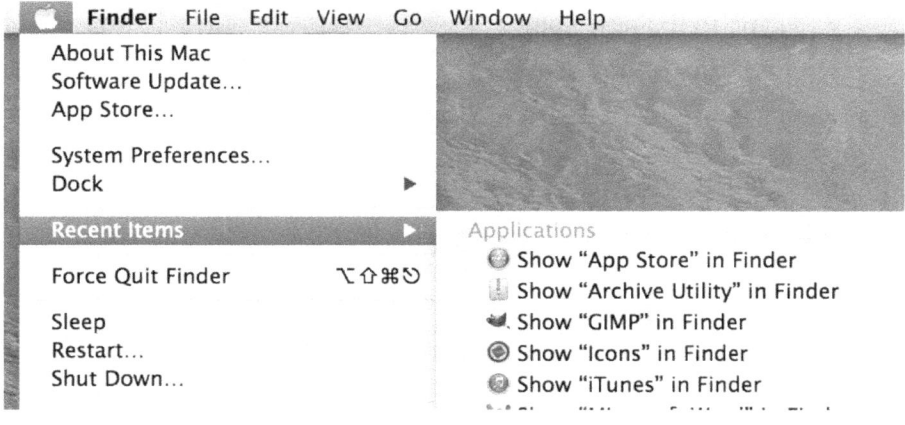

## Copy and Paste Files

To copy one or more files:
- Open a Finder window
- Click to select the file you want to copy
- To select multiple files, press control + ⌘ keys while clicking
- Select Edit→Copy from the menu bar
- Open the folder where you want to paste the files
- Select Edit→Paste

## Rename File

To rename a file:
- Click on the file name to select
- After a delay click again. The name of the file will appear in light blue. Do not *double click*. Click to select, wait a second, then click once more.

- Type in the new name.
- Press the return key.

## Finder Window Views

There are different ways you can view your files *icons, list, columns,* or *cover flow.* This is standard list view:

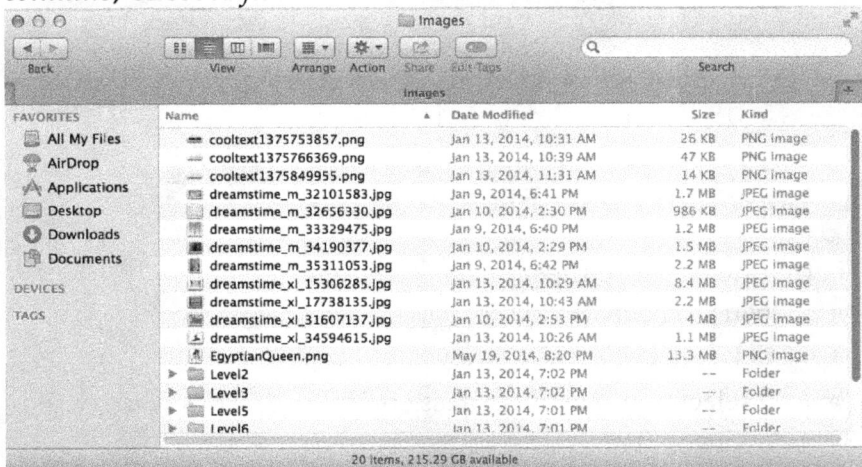

Here is view as icons:

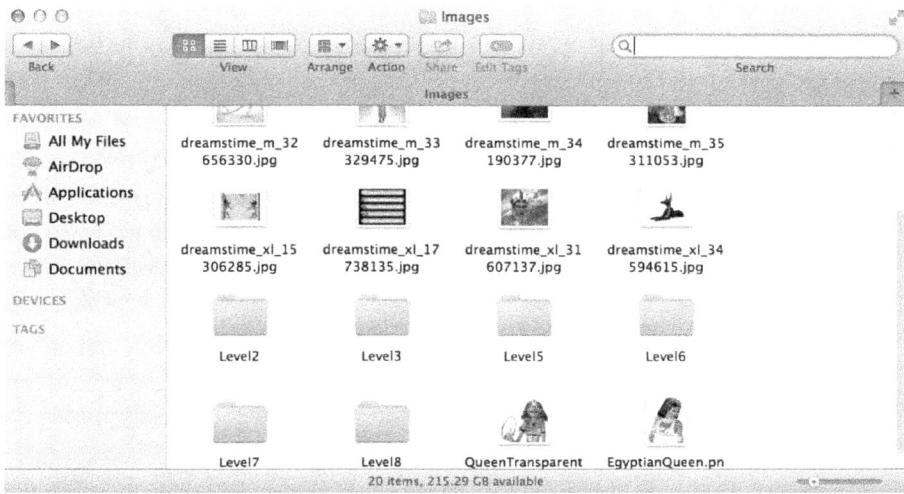

View as Columns allows you to see the overall file structure:

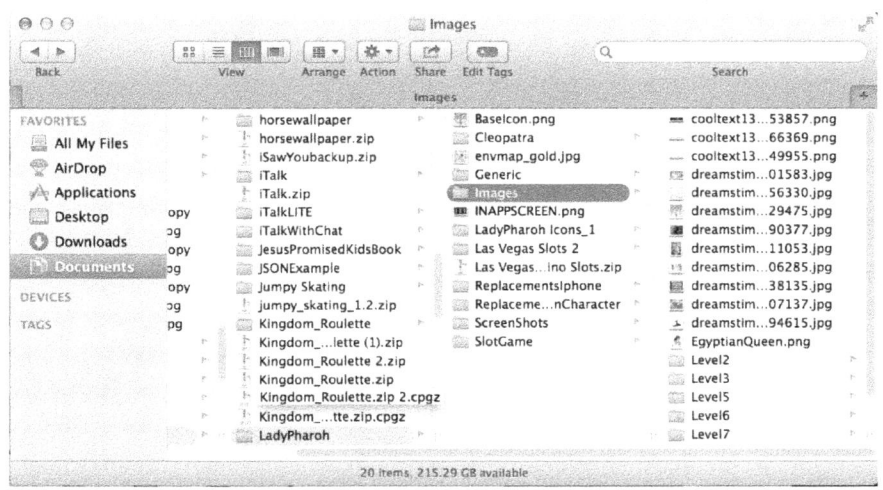

Finally we have Cover Flow, which shows scrollable icons at the top and list view at the bottom:

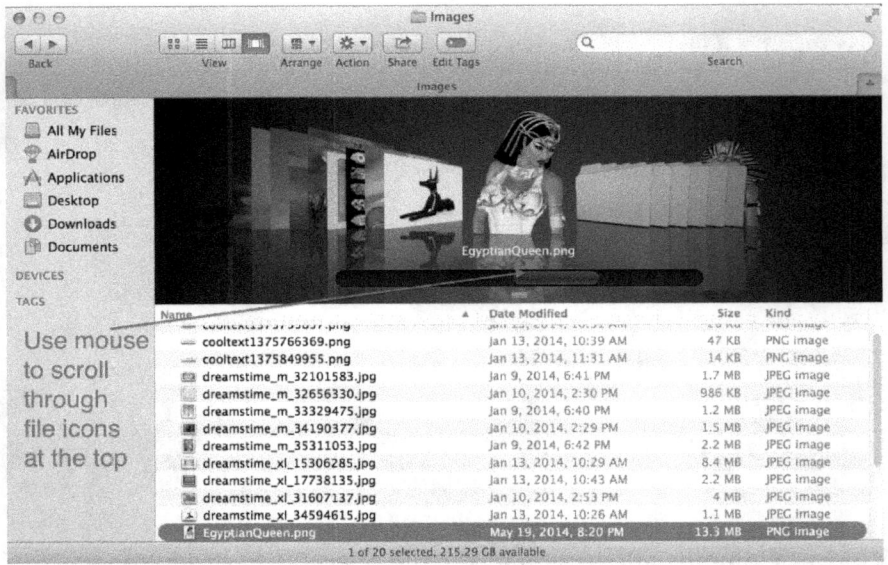

You can also scroll by swiping the images themselves using your mouse (click down with the left button while swiping).

# Chapter 3 – Keyboard Shortcuts

Keyboard shortcuts are a time saver for frequently used tasks. Individual apps may have their own special key combinations for certain tasks. You can find these noted in the pull down menus for each app, with the key combination shown to the right of each menu item. For example, here is the File menu for Microsoft Word for Mac:

| **File** | Edit | View | Insert | Form |
| --- | --- | --- | --- | --- |
| New Blank Document | | | | ⌘N |
| New from Template... | | | | ⇧⌘P |
| Open... | | | | ⌘O |
| Open URL... | | | | ⇧⌘O |
| Open Recent | | | | ▶ |
| Close | | | | ⌘W |
| Save | | | | ⌘S |
| Save As... | | | | ⇧⌘S |
| Save as Web Page... | | | | |
| Convert Document | | | | |
| Share | | | | ▶ |
| Web Page Preview | | | | |
| Restrict Permissions | | | | ▶ |
| Reduce File Size... | | | | |
| Page Setup... | | | | |
| Print... | | | | ⌘P |
| Properties... | | | | |

Commonly used short cuts that usually work with all apps include:

- New: command + N (⌘ **+ N)** Press the

command and N key simultaneously. Note that pressing the shift key for capital N is not required.

- Copy: ⌘ + **C**

- Paste: ⌘ + V

- Cut: ⌘ + **X**

- Select All: ⌘ + **A**

- Print: ⌘ + **P**

- Undo: ⌘ + **Z**

- Close Application: ⌘ + **Q**

- Close a Window: ⌘ + **W**

- Minimize a Window: ⌘ + **M**

- Eject a disk or USB device: ⌘ + **E**

- Get information about a file: ⌘ + **I**

- Search for a file in finder: ⌘ + **F**

- Open a documents Folder: ⌘ + **O** + **Shift**

- Open the Applications window: ⌘ + **A** + **Shift**

- Mission Control (birds eye view of open windows): ∧+⌘ (where the carat is your *control* key)

# Chapter 4 – Function Keys

The function keys on a Mac work as follows:

- F1: Pressing the F1 key will decrease the brightness of your monitor.
- F2: Pressing the F2 key increases the brightness of your monitor.
- F3: Pressing this key will show a birds eye view of open windows.

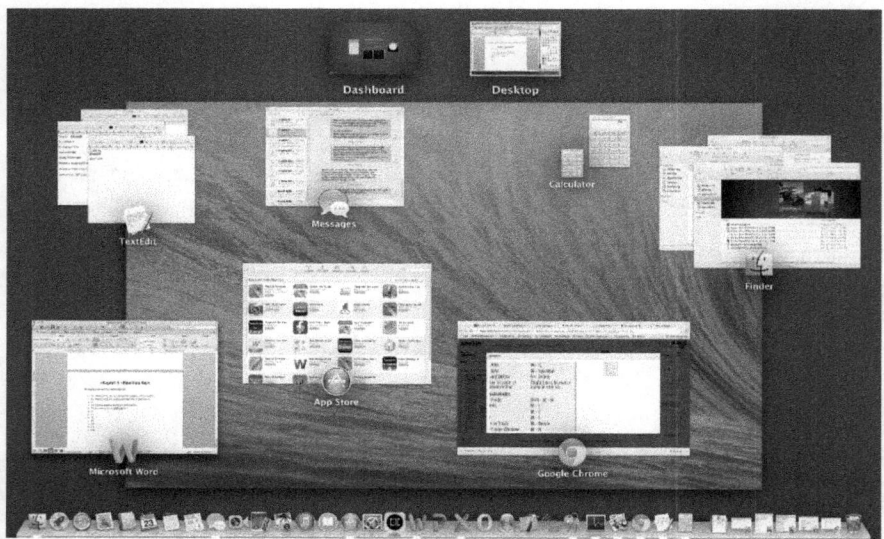

This view is called *Mission Control.* You can use this to switch between one window and another. Press F3 and then click on the window you want to have the focus.

- F4: Opens Launchpad, showing your applications.
- F5: On a Macbook, reduces the light under the backlit keyboard.

- F6: On a Macbook, increases the light under the backlit keyboard.
- F7: Media control – move to previous item in the list on iTunes.
- F8: Media Control in iTunes: Toggle between play and pause.
- F9: Media control – move to next media item in the list on iTunes.
- F10: Toggle to turn speakers on or off.
- F11: Decreases speaker volume.
- F12: Increases speaker volume.

# Chapter 5 – System Preferences Tips

The system preferences window can be opened using the pull down menu found under the apple on your menu bar:

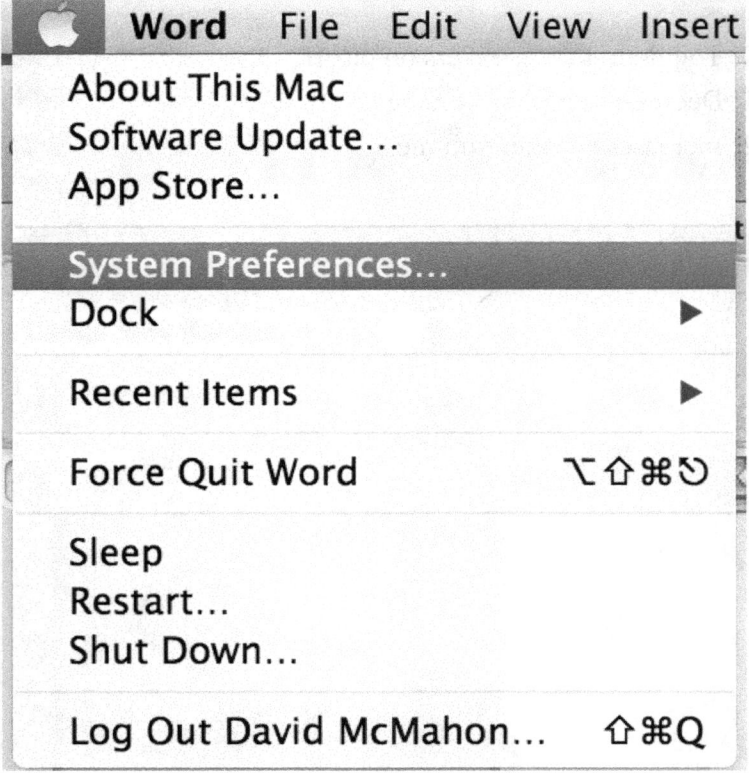

Selecting it opens this window:

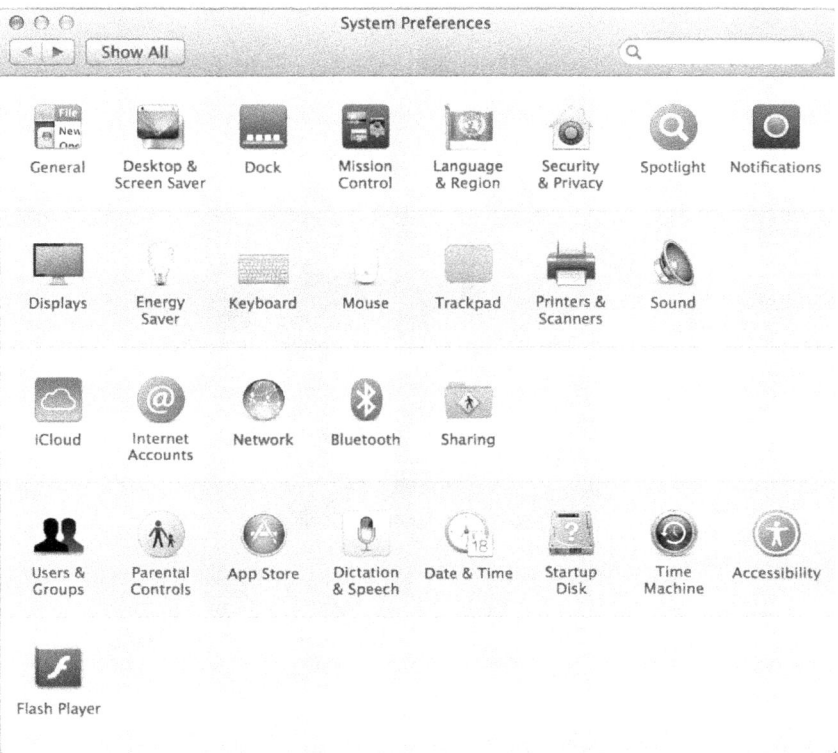

In this chapter we will review some of the most important settings.

## Desktop and ScreenSaver

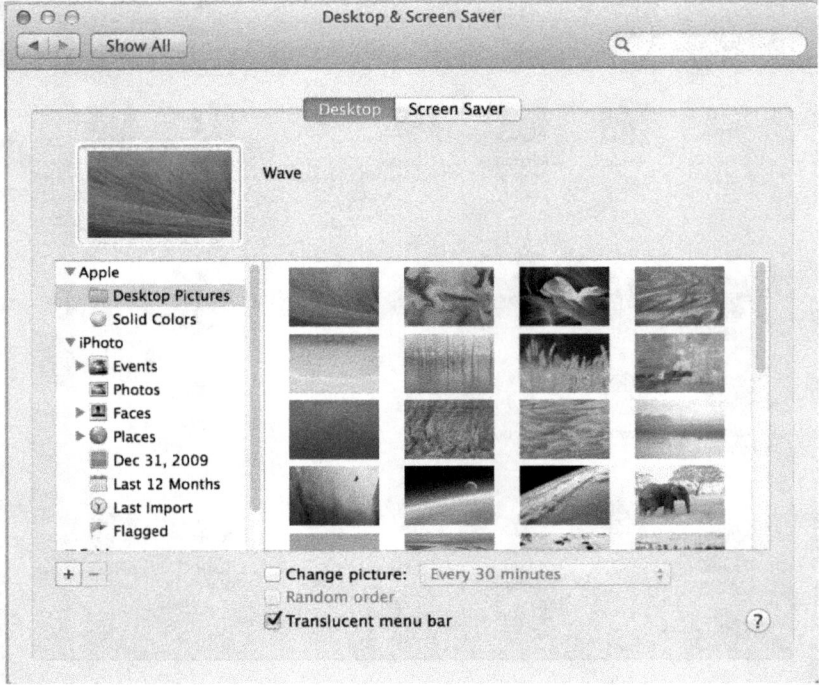

To set the image used as the wallpaper of your desktop:

- Open System Preferences
- Click on Desktop & Screen Saver
- Click on *Desktop Pictures* to use one of the images prepackaged with your Mac.
- Click on *Solid Colors* to use a simple solid pastel colored background.
- Click on one of the options under *iPhoto* to use your own images that you have imported into iPhoto, such as through your iPhone or iPad.
- Click on the + button to select a file you have saved on your computer that is not in iPhoto.

To use a screen saver, click on the Screen Saver tab. Then:

- Click open *Source* to select the source of images you want to use. You can place the images you want into a folder and select the folder as your source (select *Choose Folder* from the popup menu).
- Select the method used to display the images from one of the options shown in the left side window panel.
- Click open *Start After* and select your desired time delay after computer inaction for the screen saver to start playing.
- If you wish the clock to be displayed on your screen saver, click *Show with Clock.*

## Printer Setup

From System Preferences, select *Printers & Scanners.*

Click the + button to add a new printer or scanner.

## Parental Controls

This option lets you control children's access to certain applications and features while using the computer.

## Network

Use *Network* to set up your wireless access.

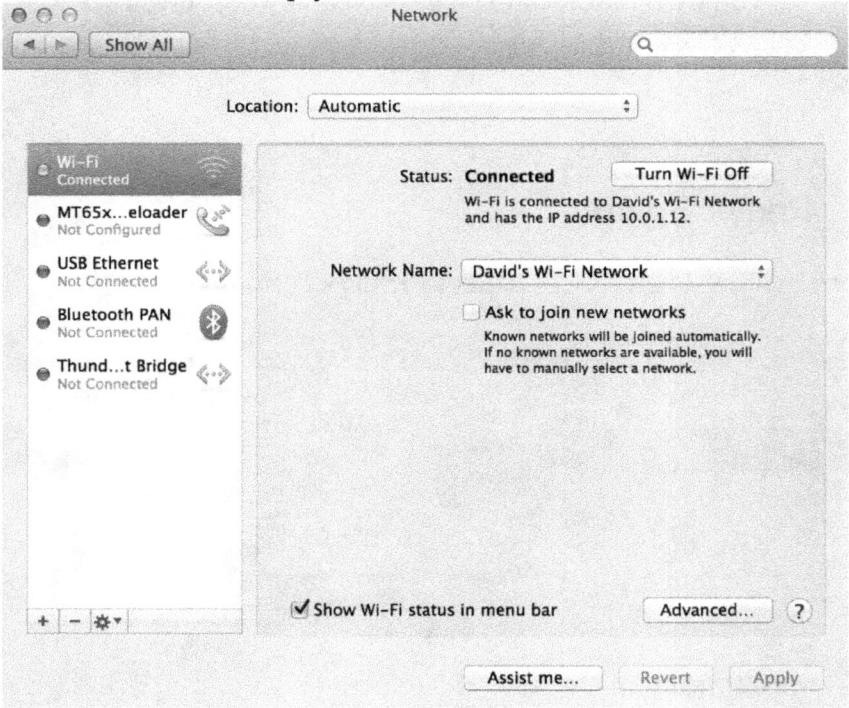

## Sound

The sound option lets you specify audio options for both input and output. For example, open System Preferences → Sound if you are using a plug in microphone for your input sound for recordings. You can also use Sound to specify where you want your audio output to go (if you have external speakers) and balance between left and right speakers.

## Mission Control

*Mission Control* is an option that gives you a birds eye view of open windows and applications. Selecting Mission Control on your System Preferences will let you set certain options such as the keyboard short cut used to open Mission Control.

## Hot Corners (inside Mission Control)

*Hot Corners* allows you to set each corner of your computer screen as a short cut to your desktop or other options. Open System Preferences, then select Mission Control, and click on Hot Corners to set up.

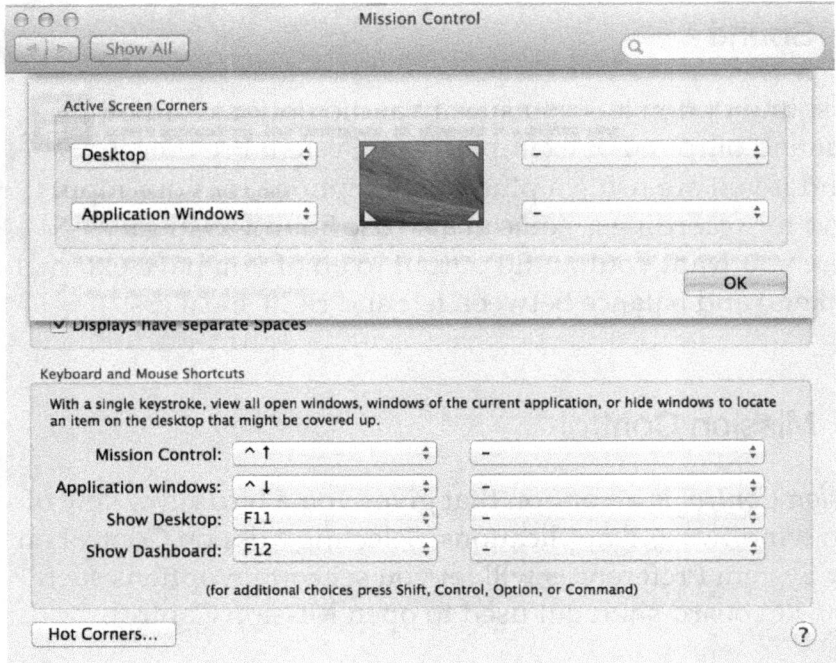

If you have set an option for a hot corner, when you move your mouse pointer to that corner the given item will be displayed on your screen.

## Startup Disk

If you want to select the disk to use for your startup disk, you can do so through the Startup Disk option on System Preferences. Typically this will only be used by advanced users.

## iCloud

If you have an account with Apple you can use iCloud for a limited amount of remote document storage. Set up your options here such as account details and which applications you want to have the option of storing on iCloud.

# Chapter 6 – Dashboard

The *Dashboard* provides a screen that by default shows a clock, calendar, the weather and a simple calculator. These are called *widgets* in Apple lingo.

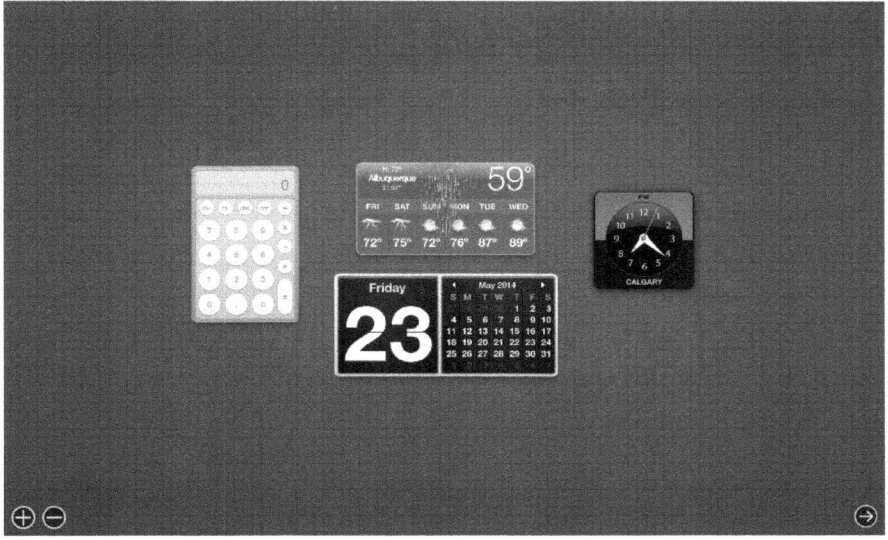

Click the arrow in the lower right corner to return to your desktop. You can add or remove widgets by clicking the plus or minus icons in the lower left corner. Clicking the + button opens this screen, which shows you more available widgets:

A widget can be thought of as a very simple application. They can do useful things, such as display stock market data or you can add sticky note reminders.

To open your Dashboard, open Mission Control by pressing the F3 key. Then click on the Dashboard icon, shown here circled in red:

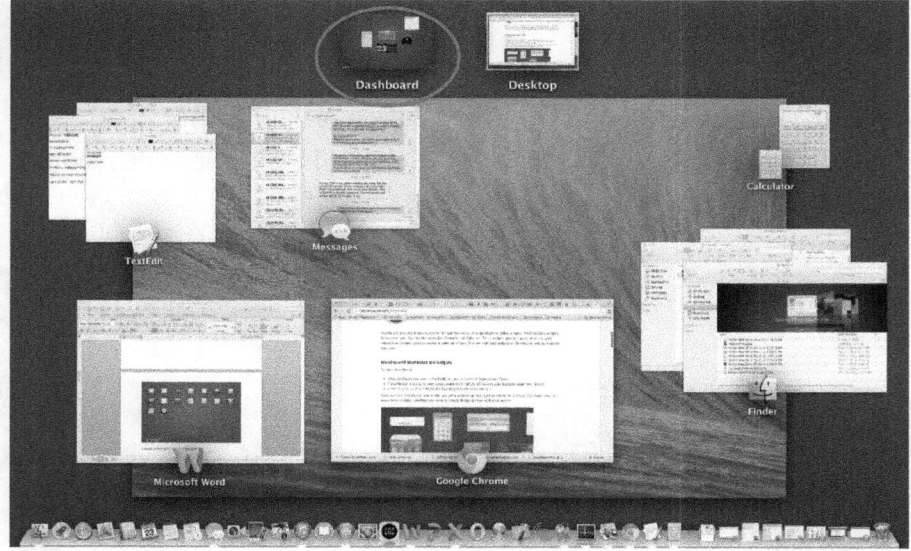

# Chapter 7 – Spotlight

*Spotlight* is a search tool located in the upper right corner of your screen. It is the small magnifying glass icon shown here:

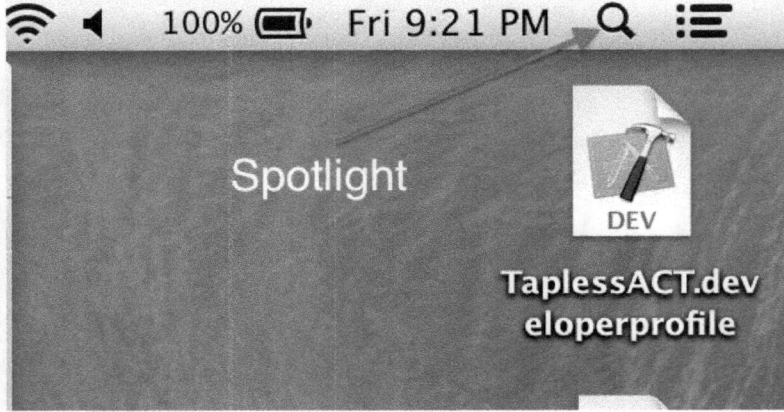

Spotlight will perform multiple search functions. You can search for an application, a file name, and even text contained within a file. To use spotlight:

- Click the magnifying glass icon or
- Press the less than key, command key and space bar simultaneously (< + space + ⌘)

Searching will also display relevant folders on your mac. Here is a search on a mac for the phrase "tax":

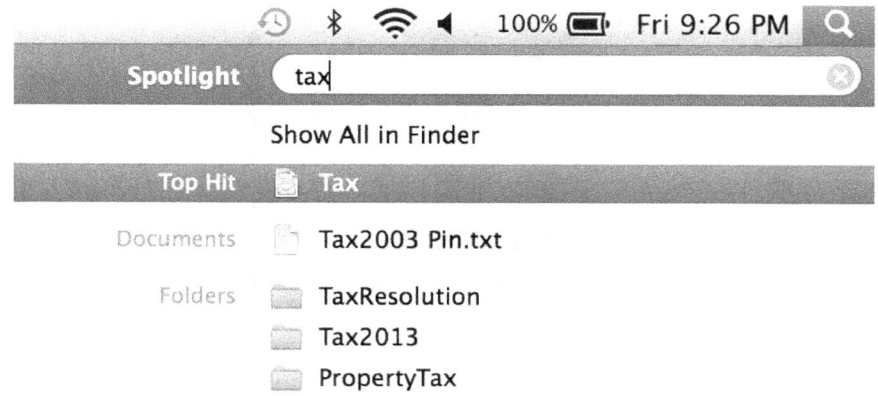

To open a file, application, or folder returned in the spotlight search, simply click on it.

# Chapter 8 – Activity Monitor

A Mac is generally a very stable computer, but sometimes you may need to force a program to shut down. Or you may want to see memory usage and other interesting data. You can force an application to quit and see CPU, memory, and disk usage by opening *Activity Monitor*. The icon for Activity Monitor is shown below:

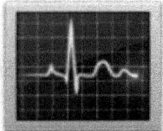

**Activity Monitor**

The Activity Monitor app is found in your *Utilities* folder, which is a folder found in *Applications*. To view it:

- Open a Finder window.
- Click on *Applications*.
- Scroll until you find *Utilities*. This is a folder. Double click to open.

Double click on *Activity Monitor* to open. The first screen will show CPU usage data for every open application and process.

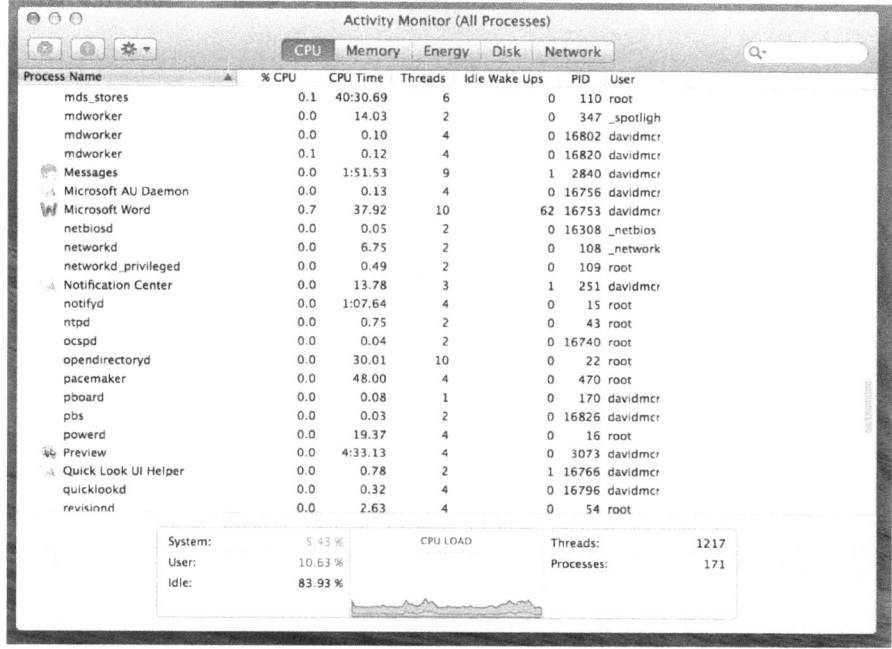

Other tabs show memory usage, energy impact, disk usage, and bytes transferred (Network) for each open application and process.

For most users, Activity Monitor will function as a way to shut down a program that is acting up or that has crashed. To do so use these steps. First, from the CPU tab, find the application or process you want to shut down and click once on it. For example, I will select Microsoft Word.

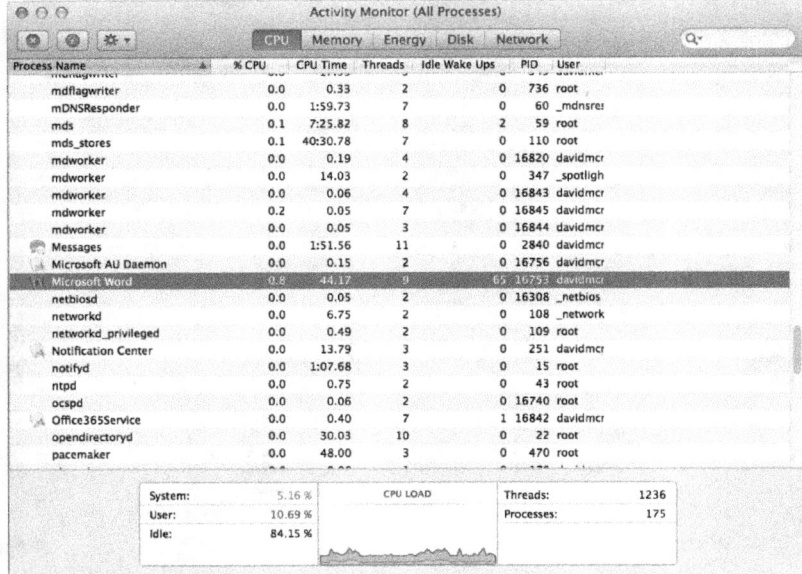

| Process Name | % CPU | CPU Time | Threads | Idle Wake Ups | PID | User |
|---|---|---|---|---|---|---|
| mdflagwriter | 0.0 | 0.33 | 2 | 0 | 736 | root |
| mDNSResponder | 0.0 | 1:59.73 | 7 | 0 | 60 | _mdnsres |
| mds | 0.1 | 7:25.82 | 8 | 2 | 59 | root |
| mds_stores | 0.1 | 40:30.78 | 7 | 0 | 110 | root |
| mdworker | 0.0 | 0.19 | 4 | 0 | 16820 | davidmcr |
| mdworker | 0.0 | 14.03 | 2 | 0 | 347 | _spotligh |
| mdworker | 0.0 | 0.06 | 4 | 0 | 16843 | davidmcr |
| mdworker | 0.2 | 0.05 | 7 | 0 | 16845 | davidmcr |
| mdworker | 0.0 | 0.05 | 3 | 0 | 16844 | davidmcr |
| Messages | 0.0 | 1:51.56 | 11 | 0 | 2840 | davidmcr |
| Microsoft AU Daemon | 0.0 | 0.15 | 2 | 0 | 16756 | davidmcr |
| Microsoft Word | 0.8 | 44.17 | 9 | 65 | 16753 | davidmcr |
| netbiosd | 0.0 | 0.05 | 2 | 0 | 16308 | _netbios |
| networkd | 0.0 | 6.75 | 2 | 0 | 108 | _network |
| networkd_privileged | 0.0 | 0.49 | 2 | 0 | 109 | root |
| Notification Center | 0.0 | 13.79 | 3 | 0 | 251 | davidmcr |
| notifyd | 0.0 | 1:07.68 | 3 | 0 | 15 | root |
| ntpd | 0.0 | 0.75 | 2 | 0 | 43 | root |
| ocspd | 0.0 | 0.06 | 2 | 0 | 16740 | root |
| Office365Service | 0.0 | 0.40 | 7 | 1 | 16842 | davidmcr |
| opendirectoryd | 0.0 | 30.03 | 10 | 0 | 22 | root |
| pacemaker | 0.0 | 48.00 | 3 | 0 | 470 | root |

| System: | 5.16 % | CPU LOAD | Threads: | 1236 |
|---|---|---|---|---|
| User: | 10.69 % | | Processes: | 175 |
| Idle: | 84.15 % | | | |

Now click the small close icon in the upper left corner of Activity
Monitor:

You will see a dialog popup in the center of your Activity Monitor
window:

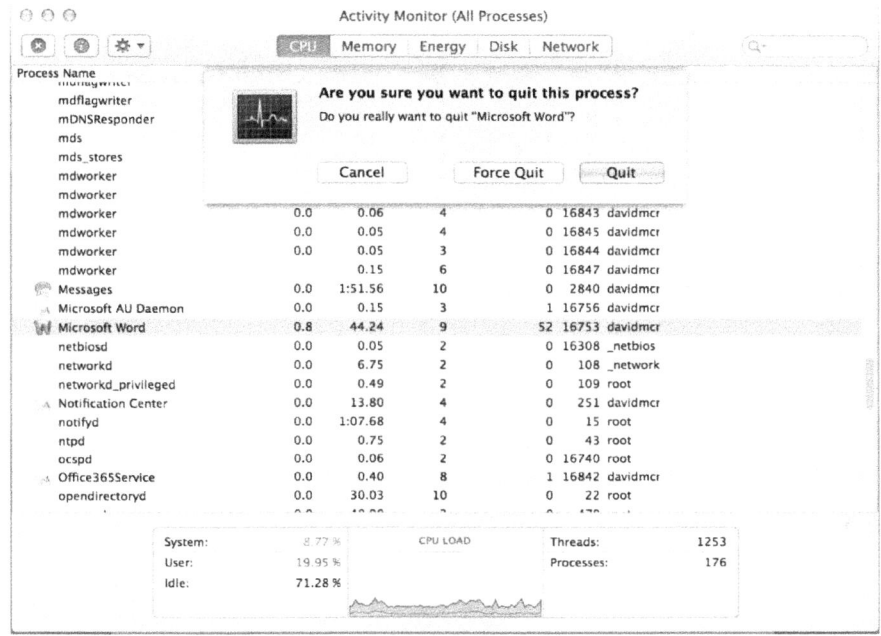

Click the *Force Quit* button. This will shut down the problematic application.

# Chapter 9 Force Quit An Application

In this chapter we explore a second way to force an application to quit. If you are using an application that freezes up:

- Press the option+⌘+ESC key combination ( where ⌘ is the command key )

This will open a small window with a scrollable list of open applications:

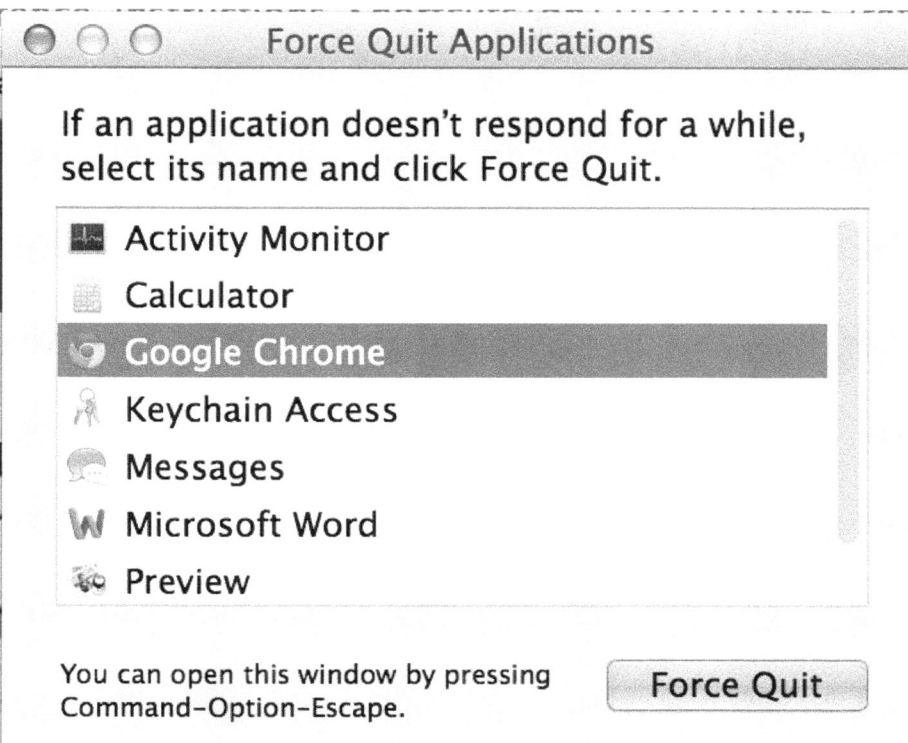

If the application you want to shut down is not automatically selected, scroll to find it and click on it. Then click the *Force Quit* button.

# Chapter 10 – Take a Screenshot

You can take screenshots using key combinations. To take a screenshot of your entire screen, press shit + command + 3. Example taken right now

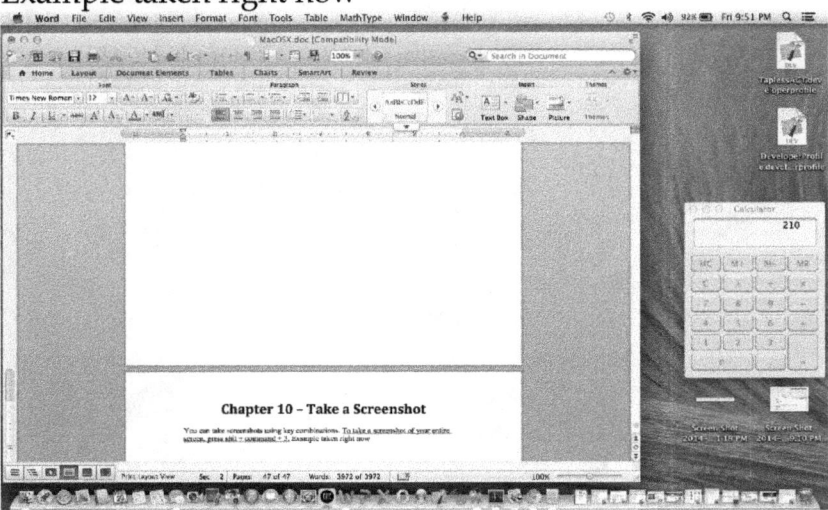

If you press shift + command + 4, you can take a screenshot of a particular region. The mouse pointer will turn into a cross hair that you can move to where you want to start capturing. Then press the left mouse button, drag until the region you want to capture has been covered, and release. Example:

## Chapter 10 – Take a Screenshot

You can take screenshots using key combinations. To take a screenshot of your entire screen, press shit + command + 3. Example taken right now

If you press shift+command+4 and want to cancel or start over, press the ESC key.

# Chapter 11 – Heads-up Display

The *Heads-up Display* provides a quick way to switch between open applications. It opens in the center of your screen and shows the application icons for apps that are currently open:

To open the Heads-up display, press the shift+command+tab keys together. After the Heads-up Display opens, you can release the tab key and the shift key – keep holding the command ⌘ key down.

Now you can use your arrow keys to move the focus from one app icon to another. When you see the application you want to use selected, release the command key. This will bring that application to the front.

# Chapter 12 – Managing Users

To manage users and groups of your computer, begin by clicking on the Apple icon in the upper left of your computer and selecting *System Preferences*.

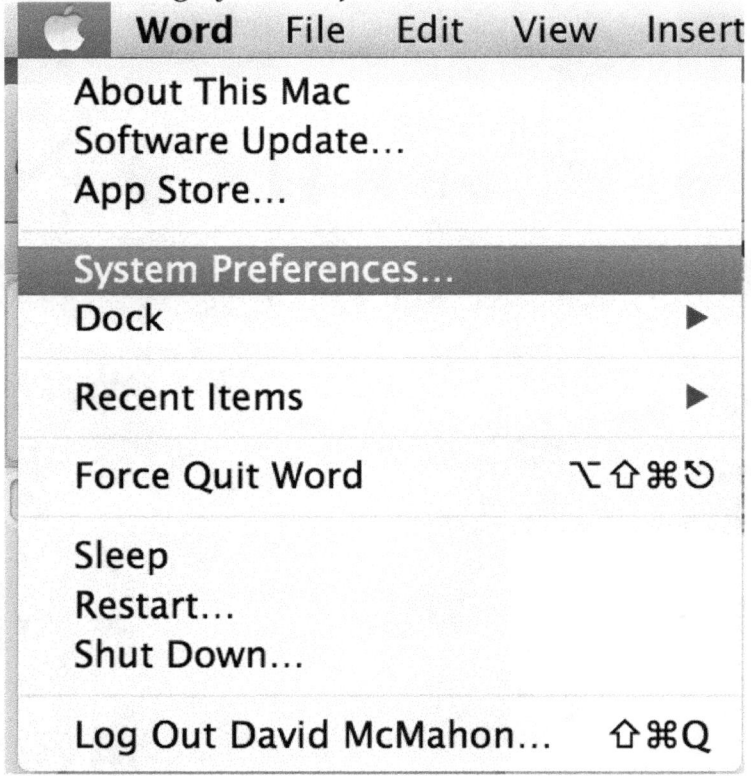

Click on Users & Groups:

This will open your Users and Groups window:

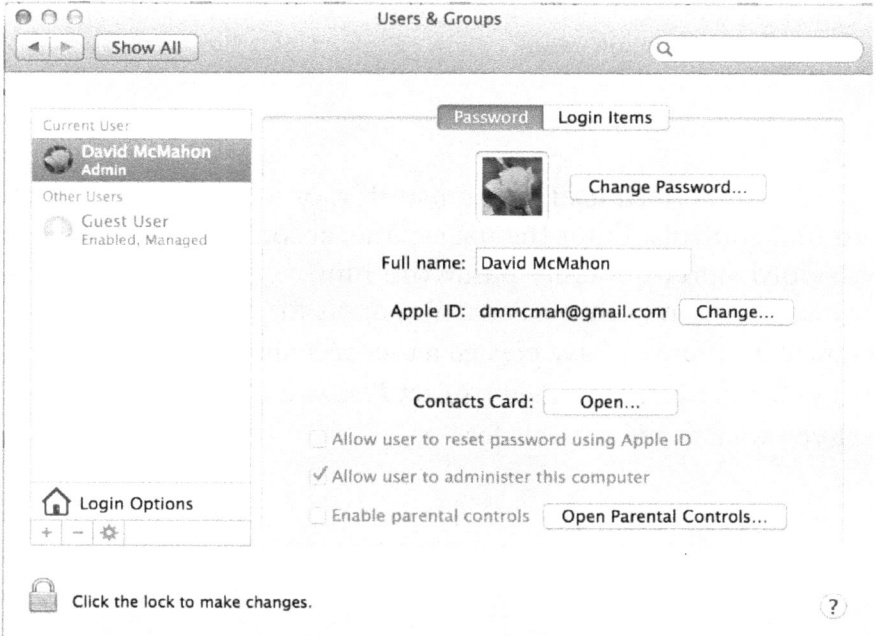

To add a new user (assuming you are the administrator for the computer), click on the lock in the lower left corner to open it. Then click on the + button. Note that a password is required to unlock.

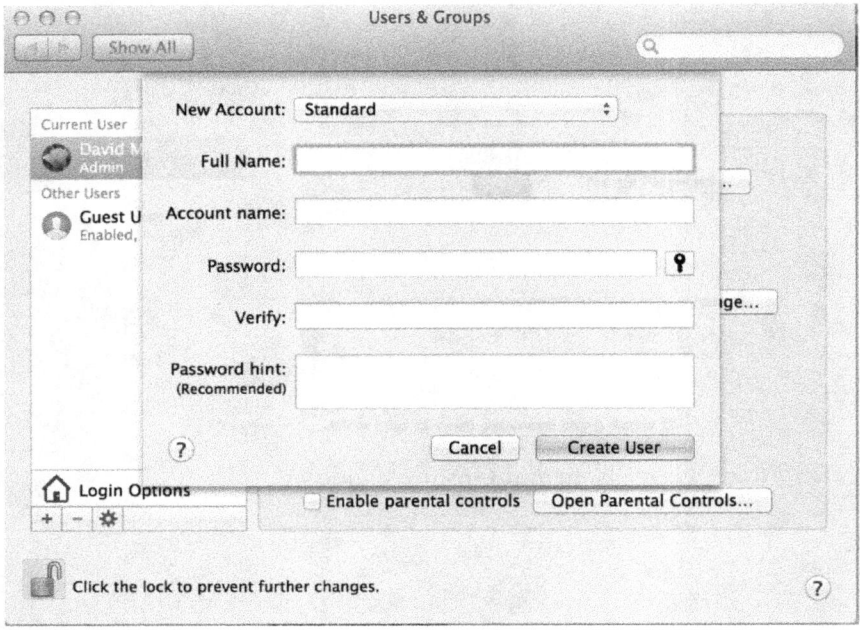

You can a standard user, administrator, or a user account with parental controls. Enter the user name, account name, and password, and optionally password hint.
Parents may want to enable parental controls for child users of their computers. After you have created a user account for the child, from the System Preferences window select *Parental Controls*. Select the user you want to add controls for.

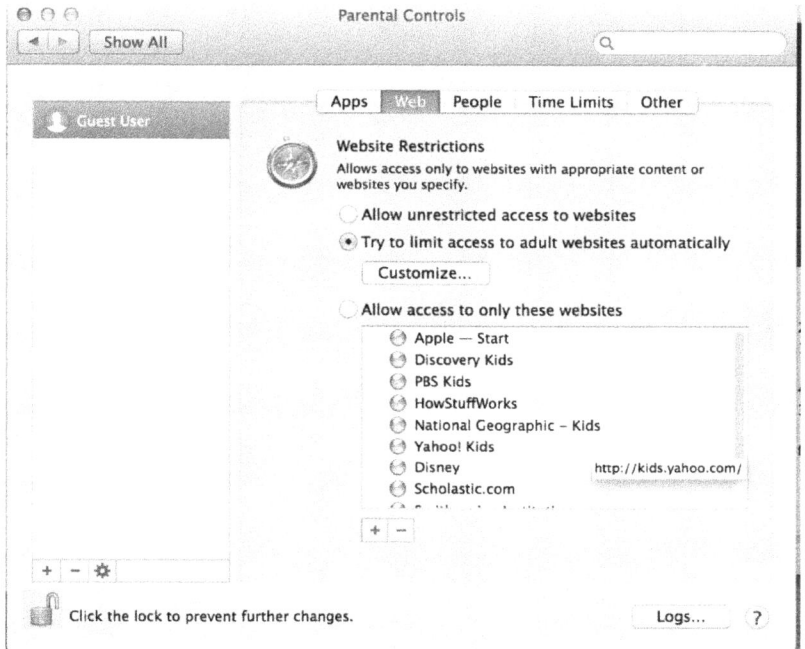

OSX allows you to add as many or as few restrictions as you desire. For example, as shown above you can allow OSX to automatically restrict website access for the selected user, or allow access only to a list of known child friendly websites. You can add a website to the list of allowed sites by clicking the + button, or use the – button to remove an undesired website.

You can also restrict people allowed for messaging, and set Time Limits for the selected user.

# Chapter 13 – Messages

The *Messages* application allows you to send and receive text messages from your Mac. The icon looks like a chat bubble:

Click Messages→Add Account from the menu bar to set up one or more messaging accounts. You can add your iPhone number so that you can include iPhone text messages on your Mac.

Accounts can also be managed from Messages→Preferences. Setting up Messages to work with chat from your iPhone will not prevent you from using your iPhone to access the same conversations. It works seamlessly with both devices giving you the convenience to chat where you are.

To send an image in a text message, locate the image you want in a Finder window and drag it into the input box on the Messages application, and hit the return key to send.

# Chapter 14- Save and Open Dialogs

The appearance of Save and Open dialogs is universal, so for this example we will use a Save dialog for the text edit application. It will open like this:

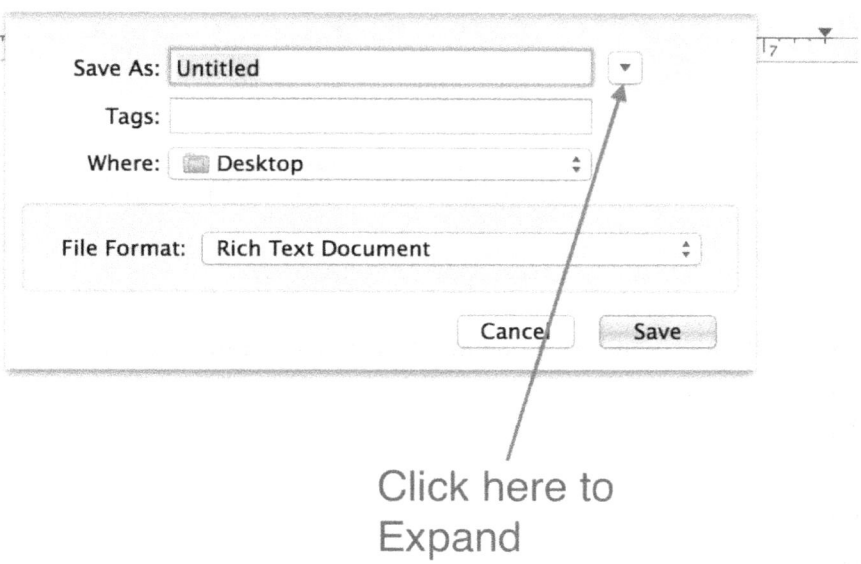

Click here to Expand

Click the small arrow to the right of the *Save As* input box to open a Finder type window:

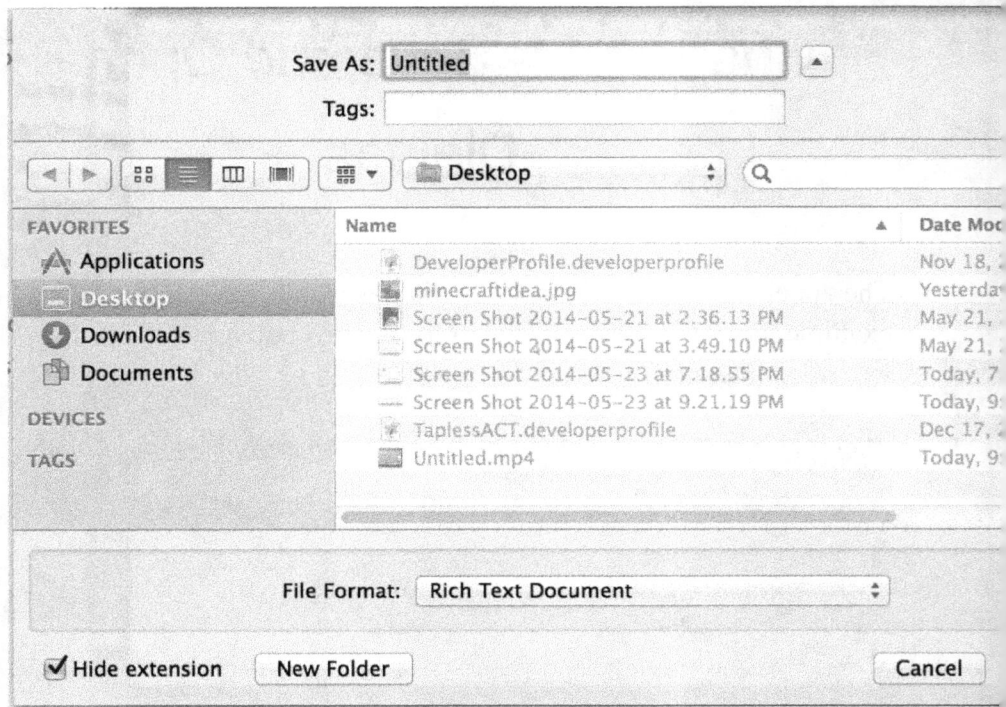

As with a Finder window, you can view items in a list format, as icons, columns, or using the cover flow interface. If saving, you can select the File Format or type, and choose whether or not to hide the file extension. If you have *Hide extension* selected the file extension will be there when the file is actually saved, but will not be displayed.

# Chapter 15-Dictation

You can use voice dictation with any app that accepts text input, such as text edit, Pages, or Microsoft Word.

To enable dictation:
- Open the app you want to use, like Text Edit
- Double tap the fn key

Your first time you may be asked if you want to enable enhanced dictation. This will require a software download:

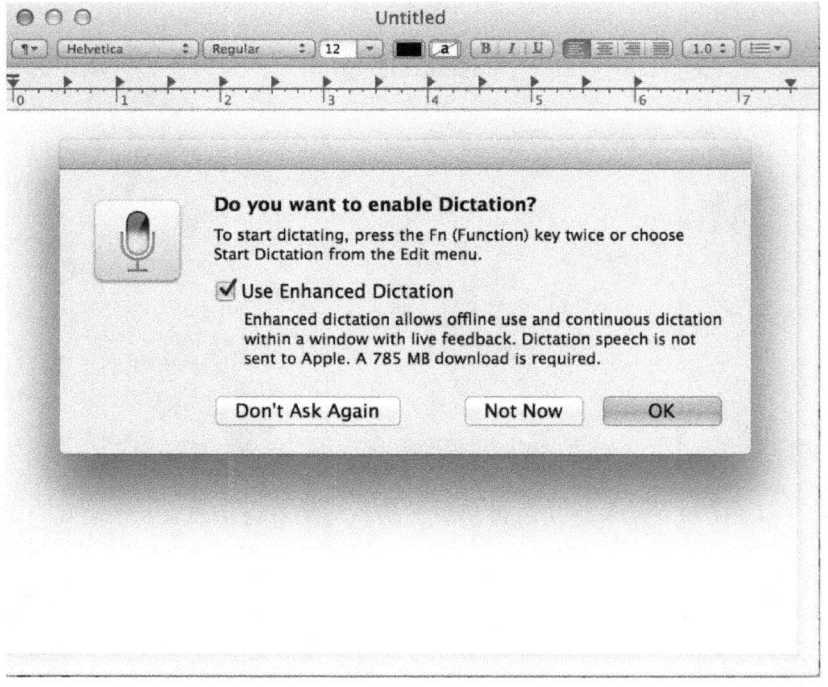

The download of the enhanced dictation software only takes a few minutes. After it downloads it will install automatically and immediately.

Alternatively to begin dictation instead of pressing the fn key twice, select *Start Dictation* from the programs *Edit menu.* Either way, you will see a small microphone icon next to your application when you enable dictation. Begin speaking and it will type what you say, as shown here:

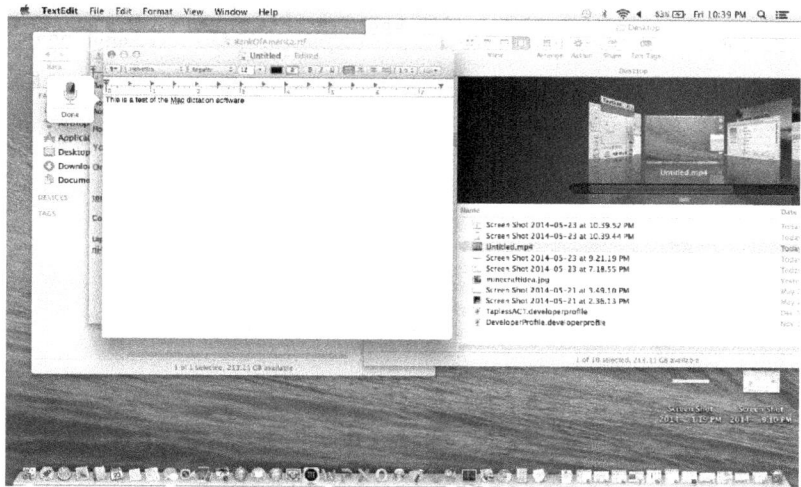

# Chapter 16- Add or Remove App to the Dock

Frequently used applications can be added to the dock:

- Open a Finder Window
- Click on *Applications*
- Find the application you want, click and hold and drag to a location on the dock.
- Wait until a space opens up on the dock.
- Release the mouse.

The applications icon will be on the dock and can be used to open it at any time.

To remove an application from the dock:

- Open a Finder window and click on *Applications.*
- Find the Application on the dock you no longer wish to be there.
- Click and hold the icon, and drag into the Applications folder.
- Release the mouse pointer. You will see a puff of smoke animation.
- The icon will no longer be on the dock, but is still accessible from the Applications folder in Finder.

# Chapter 17 – Smart Folders

A smart folder is an enhanced folder you can use on your Mac to be more organized. It can allow you to have a special folder that contains all files of a given type, for example. The folder is a kind of virtual folder – the files still reside in their real folders on your hard disk. However the smart folder behaves like a real folder enabling you to view and open files and so forth.

To create a smart folder:

- Open a Finder window
- From the File menu, select *New Smart Folder*

A tab will open in the Finder window like this:

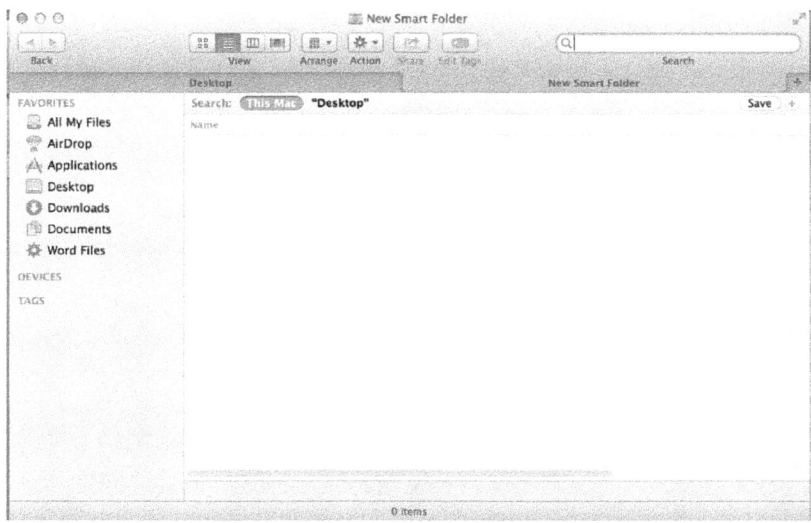

Click *Save* and name your smart folder. For this example, a smart folder named Word Files is created:

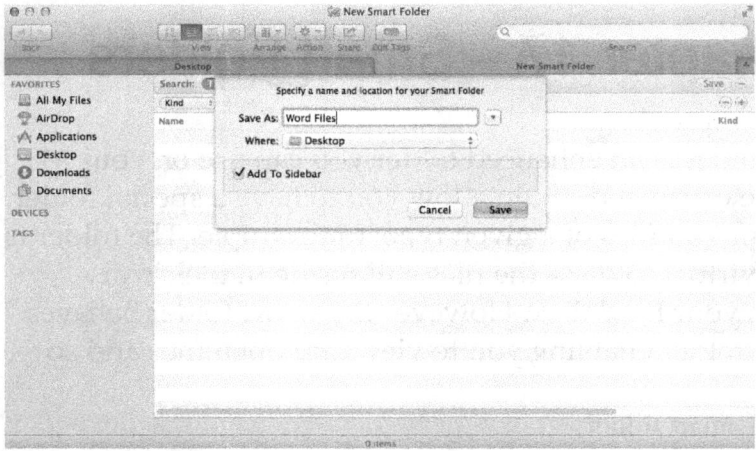

After you save a smart folder, it will appear with a purple colored folder in your Finder windows, and will also be available on the side bar:

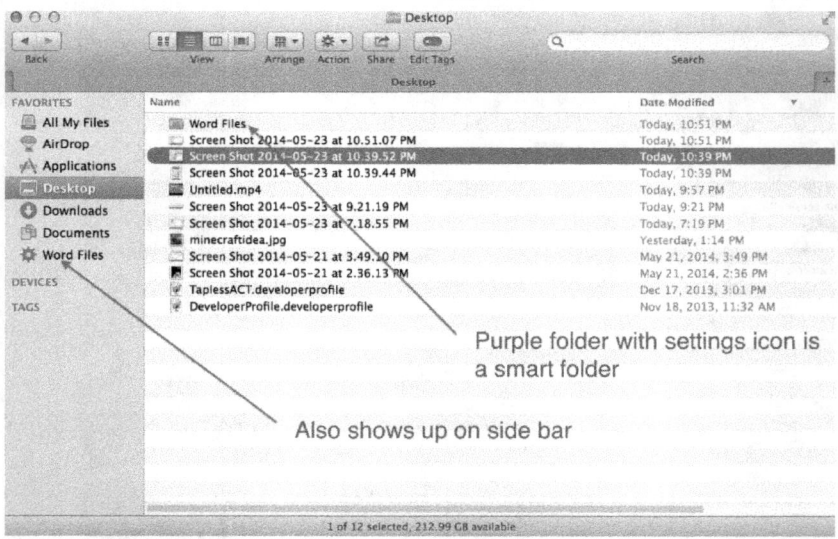

Purple folder with settings icon is a smart folder

Also shows up on side bar

To use a smart folder, click *Save*. Give the smart folder a name and location where you want to access it:

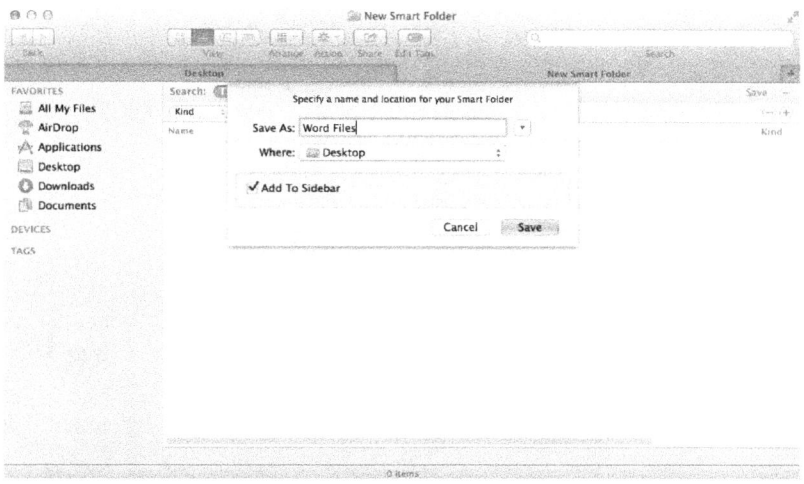

After saving it, click on *Action* and select *Show search criteria*. It will have a list of file types, you can pick one to use:

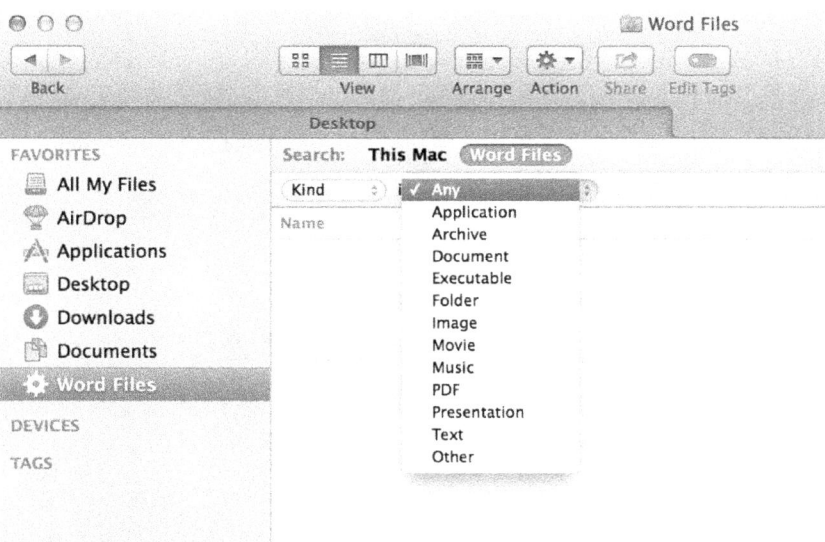

Alternatively, click *Other*. In this example we select Other and type Microsoft Word as the file type. Now we have a folder that will show all the Word documents on our computer.

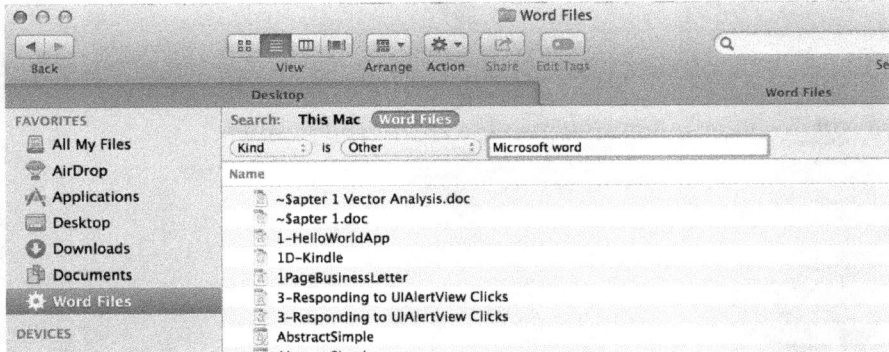

# Chapter 18- Backup with Time Machine

Time machine allows you to setup automatic backups of your hard drive. Time Machine will backup your computer every hour. It does not backup the entire hard drive every hour, it only backs up new or changed files after the first time you set it up. To get started, connect an external hard drive to your computer. Then:

- Open the System Preferences window
- Select Time Machine
- Turn Time Machine ON

Then click *Select Backup Disk* and choose the external drive you want to use for your backup. Time Machine will begin doing automatic backups, backing up your entire hard disk the first time.

After that it will only back up new and changed files every hour, as long as the external disk is connected. If you click *Options*, you will be able to exclude drives and folders from your backups. If you have a Macbook and no external drive is connected, Time Machine will create a local *snapshot* of your hard disk. You can use the local snapshot to revert to a previous state of a file.

Time Machine can also be accessed from the menu bar:

# Chapter 19- Notification Center

The Notification Center is found in the upper right of your menu bar:

It's the three bars on the right. Clicking on it will show notifications from selected apps that you set up. For example, if I have the mail app set up I see something like this:

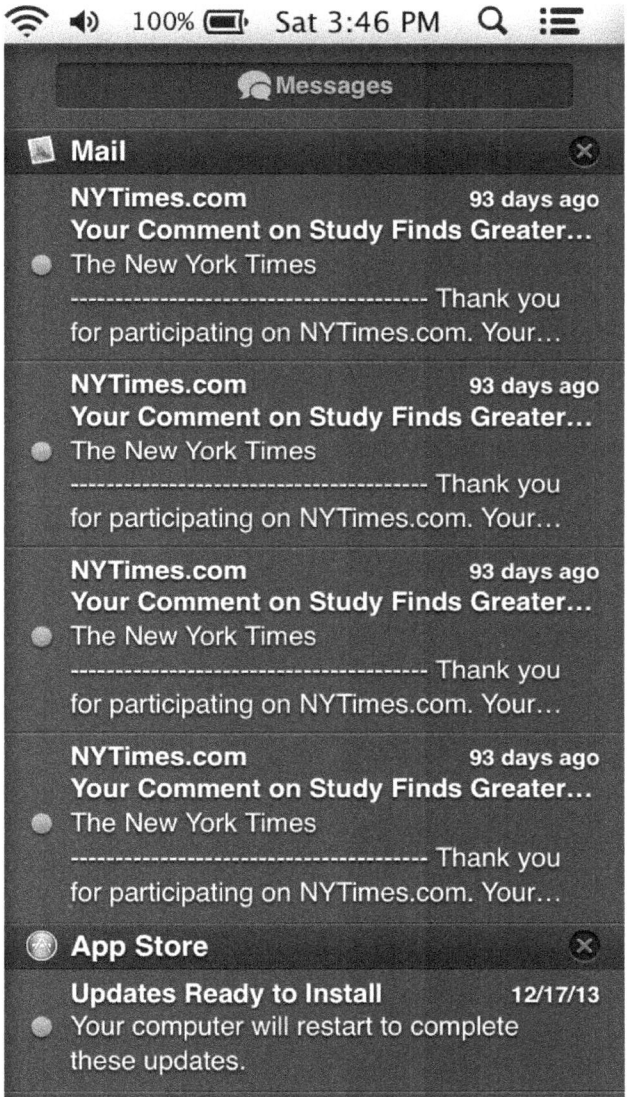

To set up which apps send notifications, click on your Apple logo in the upper left on the menu bar. Select *System Preferences* and then click on Notifications:

Here, you can set up the types of alerts if any you want each app to show you. For example, I can click on the Messages app:

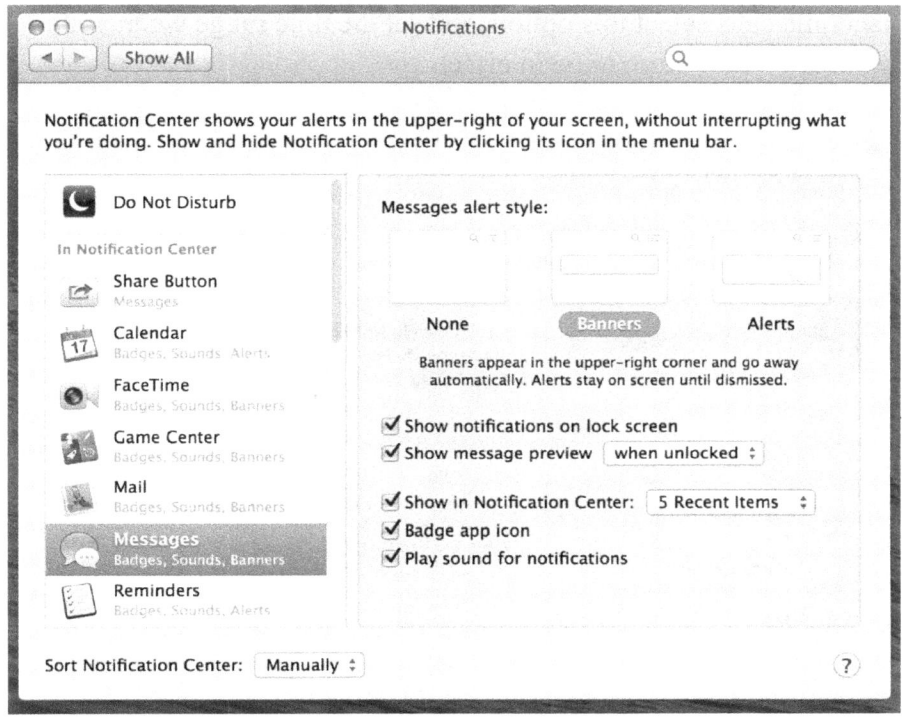

There are three types of alert style available – None, Banners, and Alerts. None is no alerts. If you select Banner, when the app sends you an alert it will appear in the upper right corner of your screen for a few seconds, and then fade away. If you select *Alerts*, the message will also appear in the upper right corner, but it will not fade away.

For each app, we also have several options such as Show notifications on lock screen, and *Badge app icon*. If Badge App Icon is selected, a red dot with a number on it will appear next to the applications icon on the dock. The number indicates the number of new messages. Users of the iPhone and iPad are already familiar with this behavior.

Finally, we have a *Do Not Disturb* option. If you are busy doing something on your computer and you don't want to receive alerts or facetime calls select this option, and set the time range when you want Do Not Disturb to be in effect.

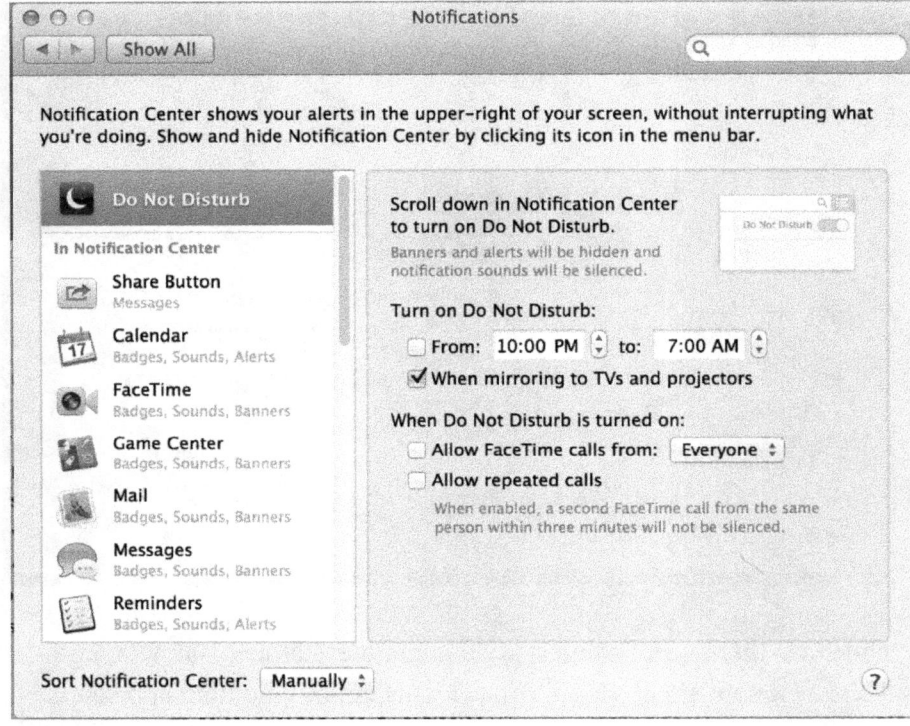

If you want to allow the reception of FaceTime calls you can check the box and set as appropriate.

# Chapter 20 – Trackpad Gestures

Many users especially those with Macbooks will have a *Trackpad* rather than a mouse. A trackpad is a nice way to get around your Mac and offers the use of gestures you are already used to from your iPhone or iPad. You can view settings along with videos of actions from the Apple Logo → System Preferences → Trackpad.

## Mouse clicks

By default, your trackpad requires a click which you can do anywhere in the lower left or right corner. A click in the right corner of the trackpad is *not* the same as a right mouse click. It functions in the same way as a left mouse click.

If desired, through the System Preferences dialog, you can set up the track pad to respond to a single tap. This is not allowed by default and honestly it takes a bit of finesse to use. When it is set up you can simply tap your trackpad with a single finger tap instead of using clicks. This is analogous to using an iPhone.

A *secondary click* on the Mac is equivalent to a right mouse click in Windows. To do a secondary click, use two fingers when clicking rather than one. The Mac is able to tell you are doing this even if you have fat fingers. This will bring up the right click or "contextual" menu.

To scroll, brush the trackpad up or down with two fingers. A single finger only moves the mouse pointer, but two fingers will scroll through your word processing document or web page.

## Pinch and Zoom

When viewing images or web pages, you can use pinch and zoom gestures that work like on an iPhone or iPad. To practice, open an image in Preview. Be sure to duplicate it before playing around with it.

Place your thumb and forefinger on the trackpad, some distance apart from each other. To zoom in, pinch in on the trackpad. To zoom out, spread your thumb and finger apart from one another.

To rotate the image, keeping your finger and thumb in contact with the trackpad, twist them either clockwise or counter-clockwise.

Be sure not to click the trackpad while doing these operations. If you are an iPhone user just use the trackpad the way you'd use your device.

# Chapter 21 – Mac hard disk organization

Let's take a quick look at the overall organization of your Mac. Open a Finder window. Here, I am in the Applications folder.

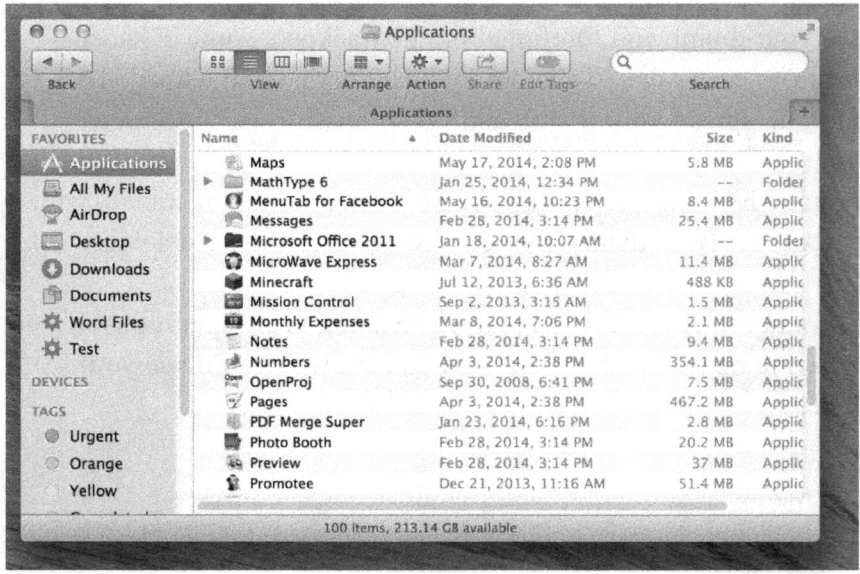

Now control click on the *Applications* label at the top of the window. This opens a menu:

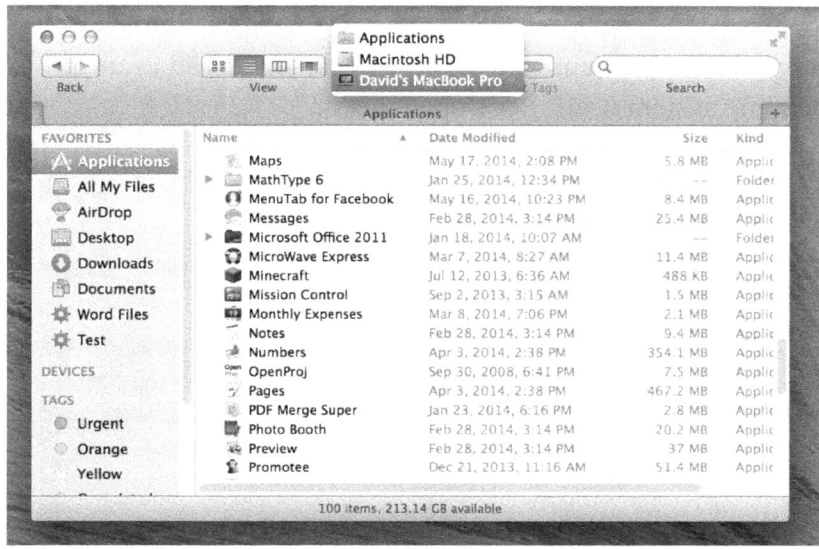

Click on your computer. This will show all drives available to the computer, including your wireless network. If you have external hard drives, they will show up here.

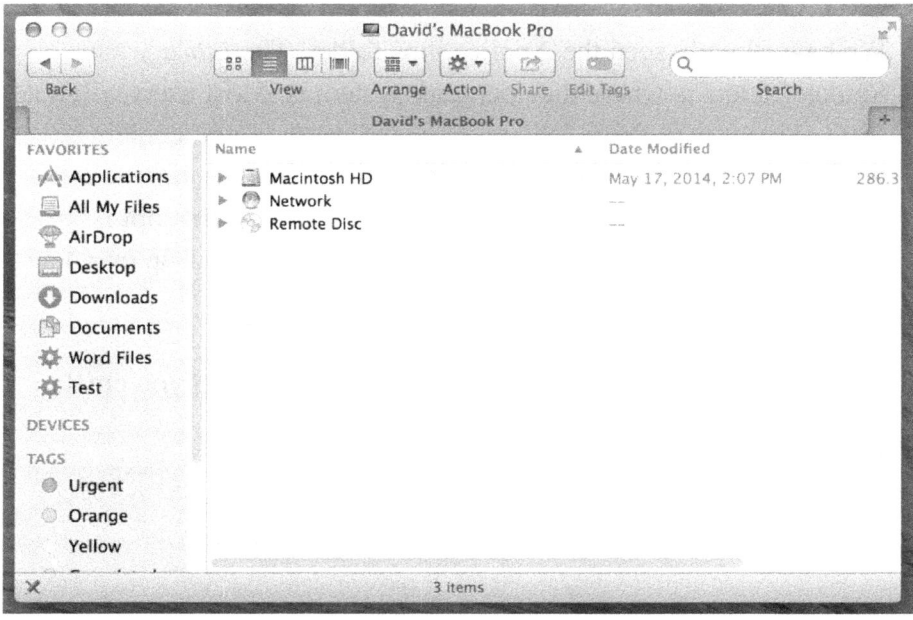

Macintosh HD is the main hard drive, which includes all users and the operating system itself. Let's open that up.

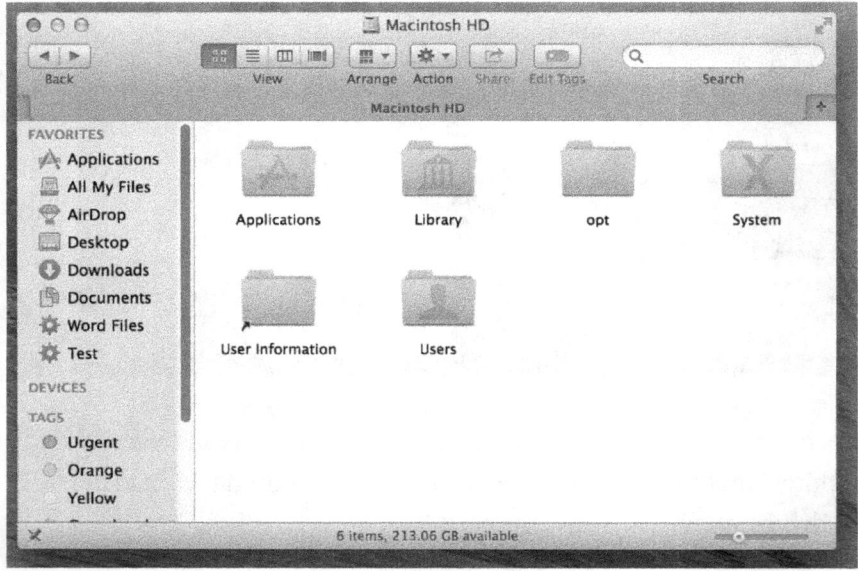

We have already seen the Applications folder. The *Library* and *System* folders is where the operating system is. Most users will not want to mess with these folders. *User information* will contain some documents that may be of interest such as licensing or instruction documents – these may or may not be present. Note that opt is specific to the computer shown here and may not show up on your system.

The *Users* folder contains all users on the computer. If you create multiple users you will see icons for them here.

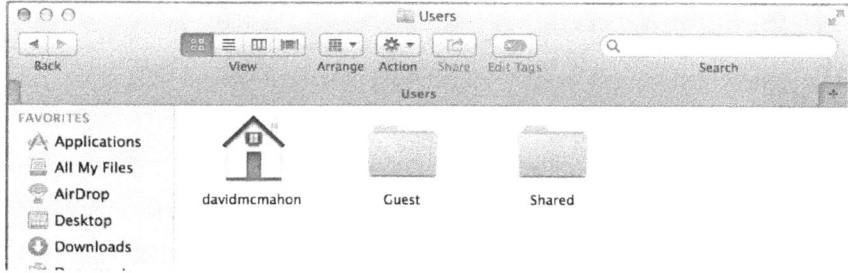

The currently logged in user has a little house for their icon (aka the home folder). Each user will have their own desktop, downloads, and documents folders. Clicking on the administrator folder we can see what a users file system looks like:

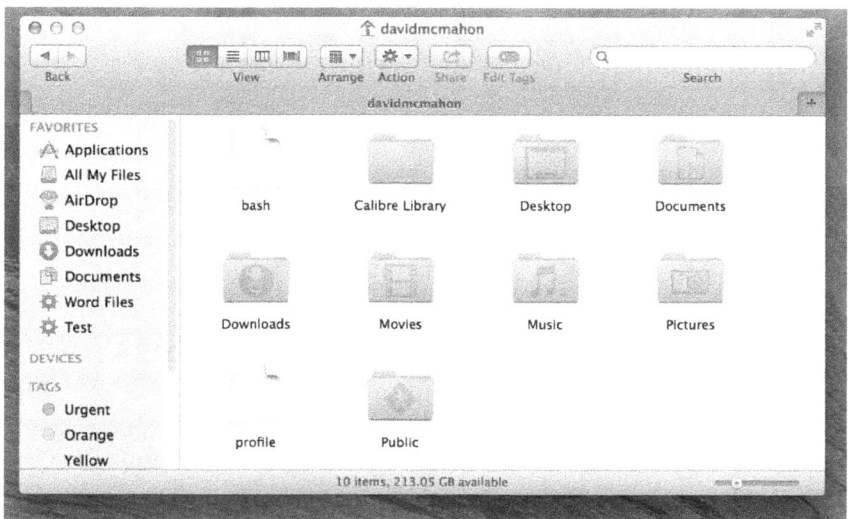

You can see that all user files specific to that user are stored here. So each user will have their own documents and Pictures files, for example. These folders are private. For example, if I am logged in as administrator and I attempt to open a folder in the Guest account, I see the folders marked by red circles. Clicking on one gives me an error message:

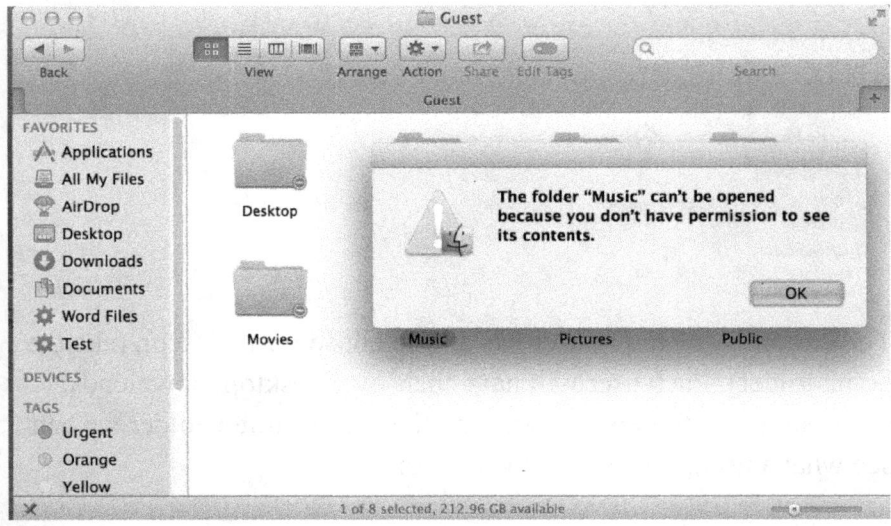

Even though this was a Guest account, you will see the same
behavior when attempting to view any users files when you are not
logged in as that user.

Any files that the user creates will be saved inside their unique
folders. So if you download an application into your downloads
folder, and log off, when a different user logs into the computer, they
will have their own unique downloads folder and will not see the file
you downloaded.

# Chapter 22 – Using Full screen Mode

Applications on a Mac can be used in Full Screen Mode. To utilize it, look for this double arrow symbol found in the upper right corner of an application window you are using:

The double arrow icon appears greyed out but will be highlighted when you move the mouse pointer over it. Click on it to enter full screen mode with the current window.

In full screen mode you will not see the normally ever-present menu bar. However you can make it appear and use it. Simply move your mouse pointer to the very top of your screen – but don't click. The menu bar will slide into view allowing you to select an item. If you move the mouse pointer outside the range of the menu bar it will slide back out of view.

To exit full screen, move your mouse pointer to the top of your screen until the menu bar slides into view. A blue highlighted double arrow will appear in the upper right corner.

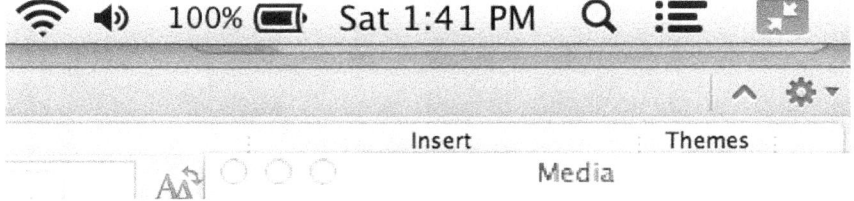

Click on it and you will exit full screen mode.

# Chapter 23 – Install and Uninstall Applications

There are basically two ways you can install an application on the Mac. The first is to use the Mac App Store. This allows you to look for free and paid apps for sale that you can easily install on your Mac. These apps are Apple approved – but this does not mean they are endorsed by Apple. It only means they have been tested for minimum standards and system compatibility. The App Store is accessed by clicking on this icon that you can find on your dock:

**App Store**

The App Store allows you to browse apps by category or top charts. You will find new releases in each category.

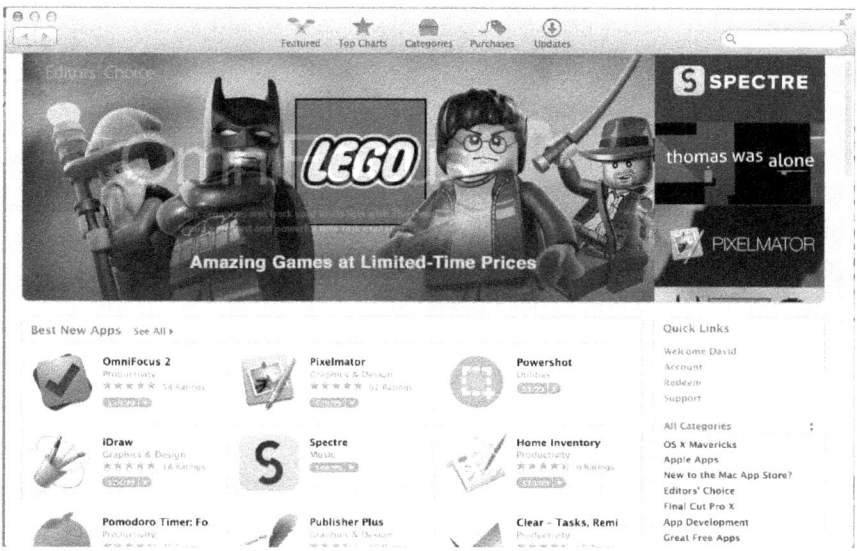

You can view details about an app by clicking on its name or icon. You can also see other offerings from each app developer. To buy an app, click on the displayed price.

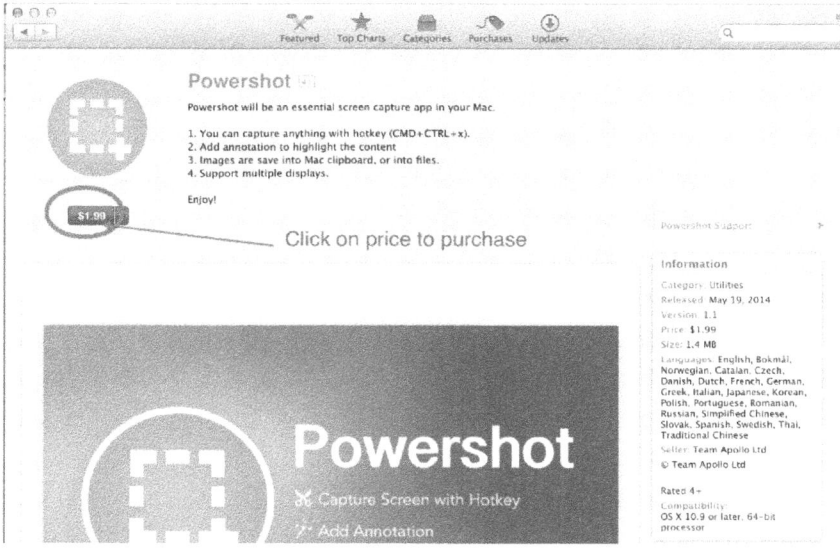

If the app is free, click on FREE. This will download and install the app. Your password for your Apple ID will be required.

You can also download and install third party applications from the internet. You do so, however, at your own risk although generally speaking the risk is quite low. Most third party applications come in DMG format. You will either be required to run an installation program, or use the following steps:

- Download the App's DMG or zip file.
- If it is a compressed file double click to unzip.
- Open the DMG file.
- Drag the icon shown into the Application folder shown in the same window.
- The app is now installed.

# Chapter 24 – Set Startup Applications and Login Options

Windows PC users are probably familiar with the *System Configuration Utility* to set which applications they want to run when their PC starts up. We can also do this on the Mac. First open your System Preferences. You can do this either by clicking on the System Preferences icon in your Applications folder:

Or by clicking on the Apple logo in your menu bar:

And selecting System Preferences from the menu:

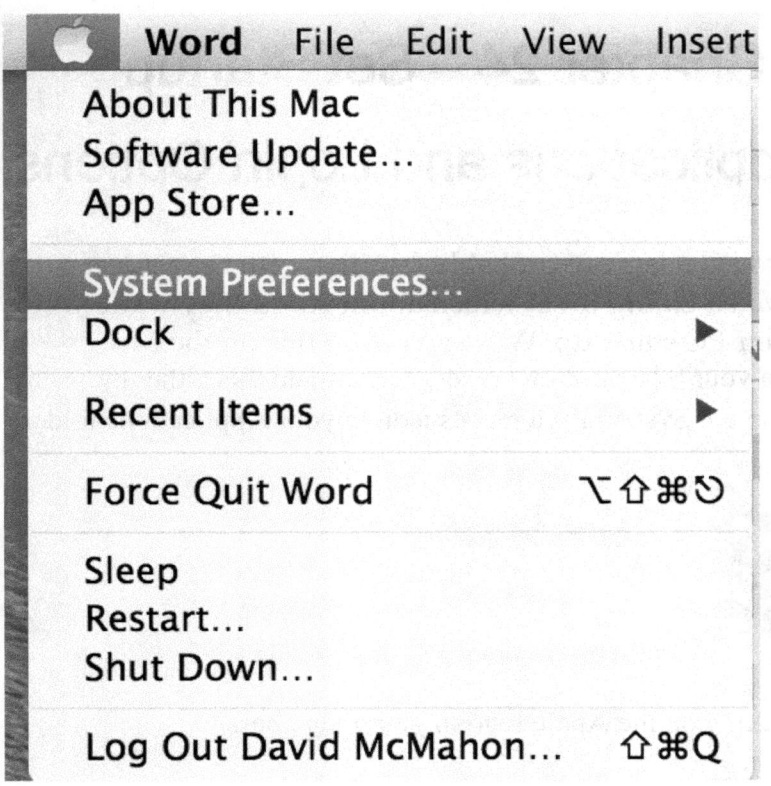

Now click on *users & groups*:

Select your user name from the list on the left side. Click the *Login Items* tab.

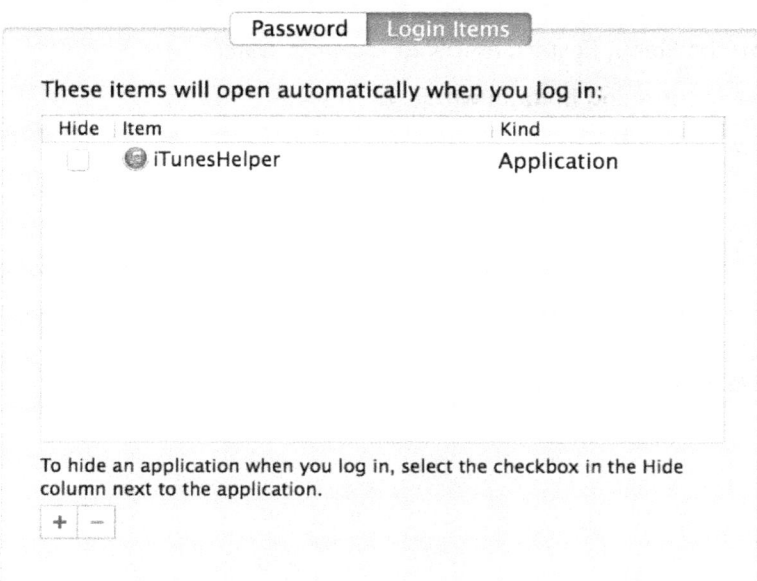

To add a new application that you want to open automatically at startup or when you log in, click the + button. To remove an application from the list click the – button. Pretty straight forward.

At the bottom of the list of users, you will see an option called *Log in Options*. You will need to click open the lock to access it.

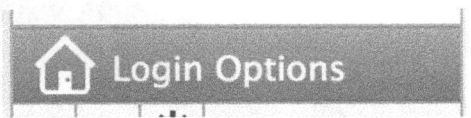

This will allow you to setup the behavior of the system when you login:

Automatic login:     Guest User

Display login window as:    ● List of users
                             ○ Name and password

☑ Show the Sleep, Restart, and Shut Down buttons

☐ Show Input menu in login window

☐ Show password hints

☐ Show fast user switching menu as    Full Name

☐ Use VoiceOver in the login window

Network Account Server:    Join...

# Chapter 25 – Set up Bluetooth

Bluetooth allows you to set up a Bluetooth keyboard, mouse, or trackpad or any other Bluetooth device to work with your Mac. As usual, we set up Bluetooth from System Preferences:

- Click the Apple Logo
- Select System Preferences from the drop down menu
- Click on Bluetooth

The System Preferences window will show a list of connected devices and give the option to turn Bluetooth off.

Connecting a device is simple.

- Turn on the device.
- Open Bluetooth from System Preferences.
- Make sure your computer is in "discoverable" mode. If you don't se "Discoverable mode" on the screen, click the *Turn Bluetooth On* button.
- Find the device in the list of Bluetooth devices.
- Select the device.
- Click the Pair button.

Devices can also be deleted by clicking the X to the right of the Device name.

Bluetooth can be accessed from the right side of the menu bar:

If you have a Bluetooth device connected to your computer they will show up in this menu. This allows you to send files to or browse files on a device. You can also turn Bluetooth off, or open Bluetooth preferences from this location.

# Chapter 26 – Contextual menu

A *contextual menu* is just a popup menu that appears under your mouse cursor. It is called a contextual menu because the content of the menu depends on the context in which it is opened.
For example, we can open a contextual menu from the desktop.

To open a contextual menu on your desktop, press the control key and then click with your trackpad. Here we see that we can change desktop background or open a new folder among other options. To see how it operates differently depending on the context, let's press control + click while inside a finder window. Now we see this popup menu, which is suitable to managing files inside the finder window:

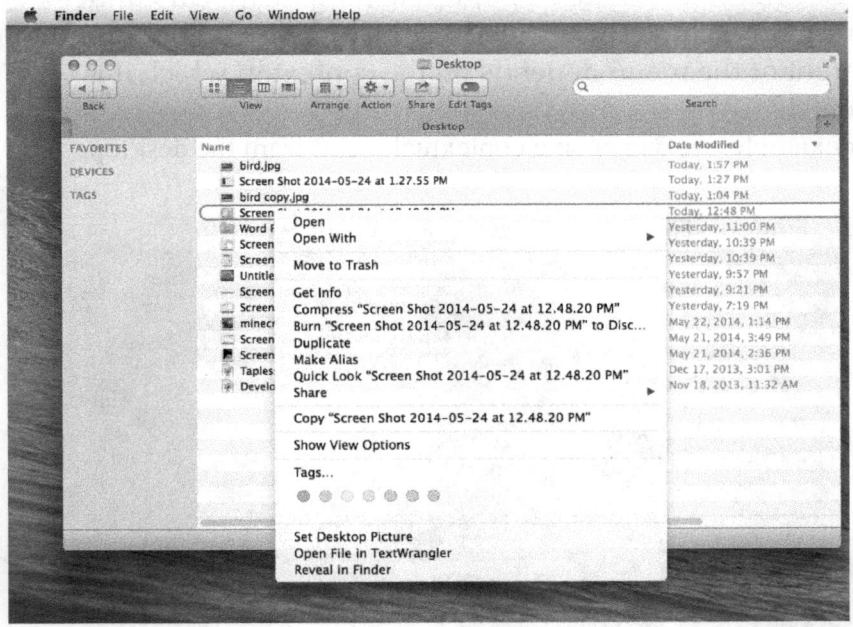

## Opening Contextual Menus with a Mouse

If you are using a multi-button mouse with your Mac, you can set up the right mouse button to work like a right mouse click in Windows. That is, to bring up the contextual menu. To do this click on the Apple logo in the upper left of your screen, and select System Preferences. Then click on Mouse. A diagram of your mouse along with popup menus for the function of each button will open. Select *Secondary Button* for the right mouse button to have your mouse open contextual menus with your right mouse click.

# Opening Contextual Menus with a Trackpad

By default, a trackpad is set to open contextual menus with a click with two fingers. So simply click on the trackpad with two fingers and it will work the same as control + click. You can also change this to open the contextual menu with a click in the lower left or right corner. To do this click on Apple Logo, select System Preferences, select Trackpad, and click open the drop down menu for secondary click.
Note that no matter what options you set, control + click will always open the contextual menu.

# Chapter 27 – Tags in Detail

In Mac OSX Mavericks you can apply multiple tags or labels to a document. This will help you search for files. Tags on files are indicated with colored dots.

Let's see how you apply a tag. Here I open a Finder window:

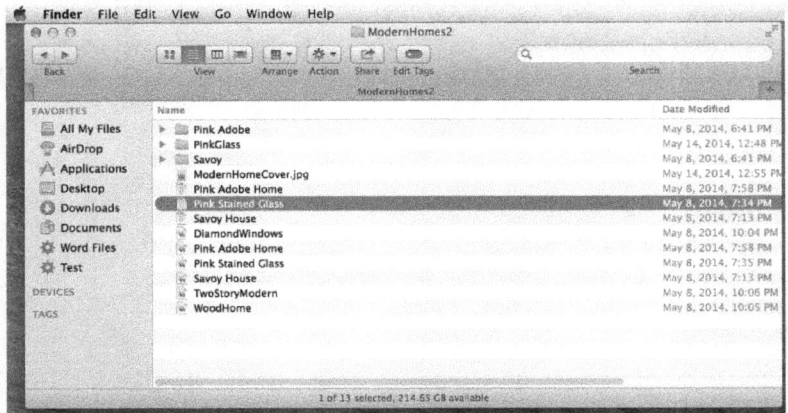

Tags are shown by default as colors. For example we can add a blue tag to the file "Pink Stained Glass". Press control+click and move your mouse pointer over tags, and click on the blue tag. Now we see it like this:

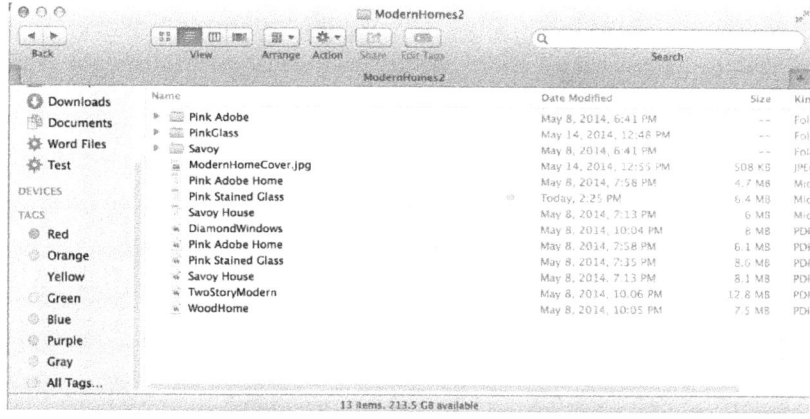

Now we can search for all files on our Mac that have a blue tag. In a spotlight box, type "blue"

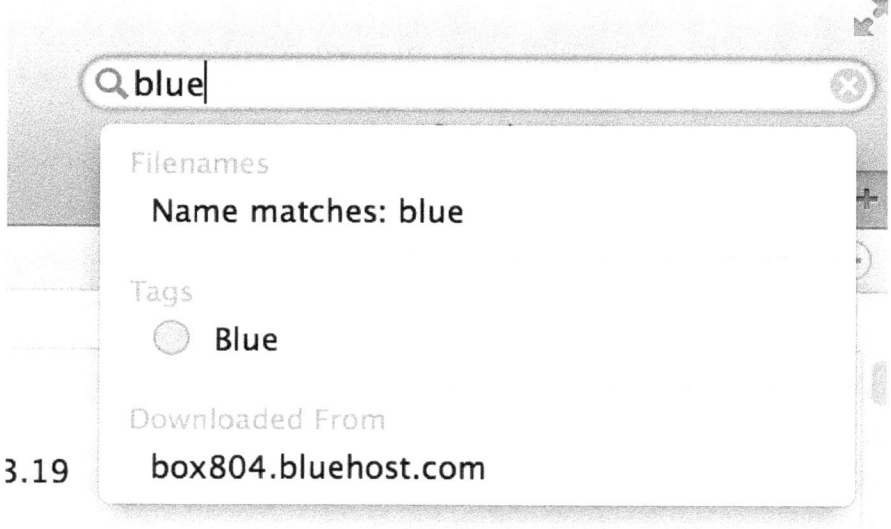

3.19

Click on Blue under Tags. This will show all files that have been tagged "Blue" will be displayed in your Finder window.

While this may be useful, you probably want to give your tags personal meanings. With a Finder window open or from the desktop, click on Finder→Preferences. Then click on the tags tab.

We can change the name associated with each tag. Just click and type on the name. For example, I can change Red to Urgent, and Green to completed.

# Chapter 28 – Built-In Apps

Your Mac comes with several built-in apps that are quite useful. We summarize them here.

**Text Edit**

A rich text editor. More sophisticated thatn Microsoft Notepad, this app is more equivalent to wordpad.

TextEdit

**Calendar**

Calendar is a relatively sophisticated calendar app showing daily, weekly, monthly, and annual views. You can add events to a given day and holidays are denoted on the calendar.

Calendar

You can create a "Quick Event" by clicking on the + sign in the upper left corner, or double click on a date to create an Event and add attendees.

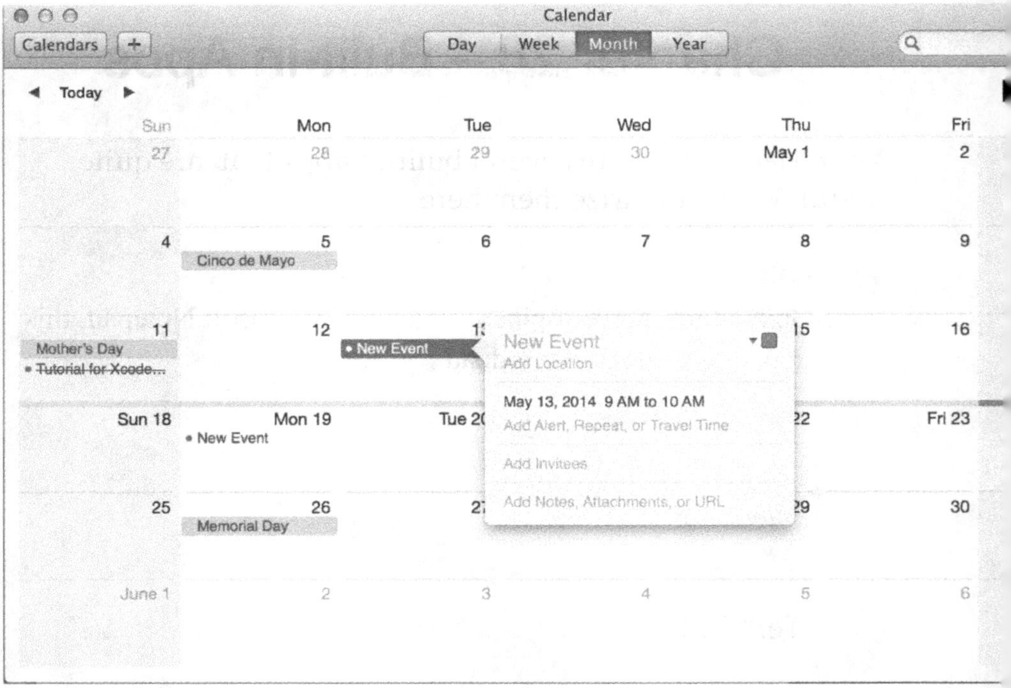

Calendar screenshot showing Month view for May 2014 with a New Event popup.

## iMovie

iMovie is Apple's famous personal movie editing software. You can open it from the dock by clicking this icon:

iMovie

## iPhoto

For managing your files – in particular photos and videos from your iPhone and iPad, you will use iPhoto. After your Mac has been set up to work with your device when you plug in your iPhone or iPad, iPhoto will open automatically. It will give you the option to import new photos from your device. At the very least, it provides an automatic backup of images (and videos) on your device. You can then export images from iPhoto to locations on your hard drive or use them directly in documents created with Pages, Keynote, or Microsoft Word and Powerpoint, for example.

iPhoto

**iTunes**

iTunes is the famous media app put out by Apple. It is automatically installed on your Mac. It allows you to play and manage your music files, as well as video including movies and TV shows you can rent or buy in the iTunes store.

iTunes

**Mail**

Mail is a built in email application that can be set up with various email accounts.

**Mail**

## Notes

Notes is an application that allows you to keep time/date stamped notes.

**Notes**

## Reminders

A step up from Notes, Reminders does what it says – allowing you to set a reminder for yourself on a date/time or at a specific location.

**Reminders**

## Time Machine

Time Machine allows you to back up your hard disk or if you have a Macbook to make a local copy of your files. Time machine is an important app so please see the chapter on setting it up.

Time Machine

# Chapter 29 – Using Preview and Duplicating Files

*Preview* is a built-in app that you can use for viewing photos and PDF files. In addition to viewing, Preview allows you to do minor edits and annotations to your images, and to export them as new files. Preview is also a good example of autosave, a feature that can be annoying on the Mac if you aren't too careful.

## Duplicate and care with Autosave

If you just go and edit a file you may find that the changes you made were saved regardless of whether you intended it or not. Note that this is only true with Apple applications and is probably not true with third party applications like Microsoft Word that still use "Save" and "Save As".
To make sure that doesn't happen to your documents, use the following procedure. First double click on an image to open with Preview.

Preview offers the ability to adjust colors, change file types, brightness and contrast among other things. Let's turn this into a black and white image – but being careful not to overwrite the original. First *duplicate* the image. Select File→Duplicate or with the image selected in Preview press shift + command + s:

This creates an exact copy of the image:

This allows you to work on the copy without doing anything at all to the original. In fact we can close the original at this point by clicking

on its close button .

To see what types of edits are available, click open the *Tools* menu. This has many options such as adjusting the size of the image, rotating it, or adjusting colors.

For this example we will create sepia version of the picture. When you select Adjust Color this dialog opens:

Dragging the Sepia bar all the way to the right, we have a Sepia version of the image.

Notice that you can select *Reset All* at any time to return to the original version of the image. Clicking the close icon in the top left of the Adjust Color dialog will dismiss the window and keep the changes. Now we can save the file. Click the File pull down menu and select *Export*.

Notice that the File pulldown menu has options *Export as PDF* and *Revert*. The Revert To option is only available when working with an original image. Selecting Export opens a dialog allowing you to select image output type (JPG, PNG etc.) as well as file name and location:

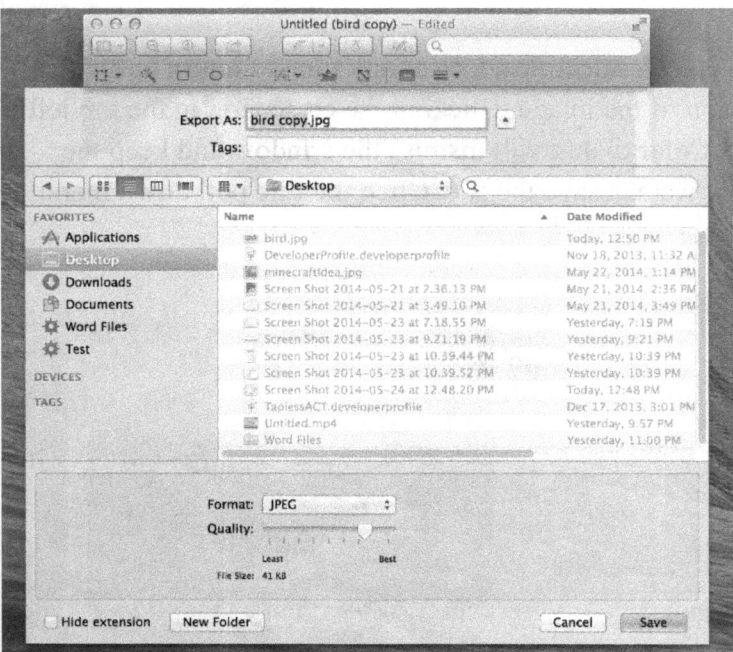

# Annotating Images and PDF Files

Preview has a handy and easy way to annotate files. Select Tools→Annotate for options that allow you to add a line/arrow, oval, square, or text to the image.

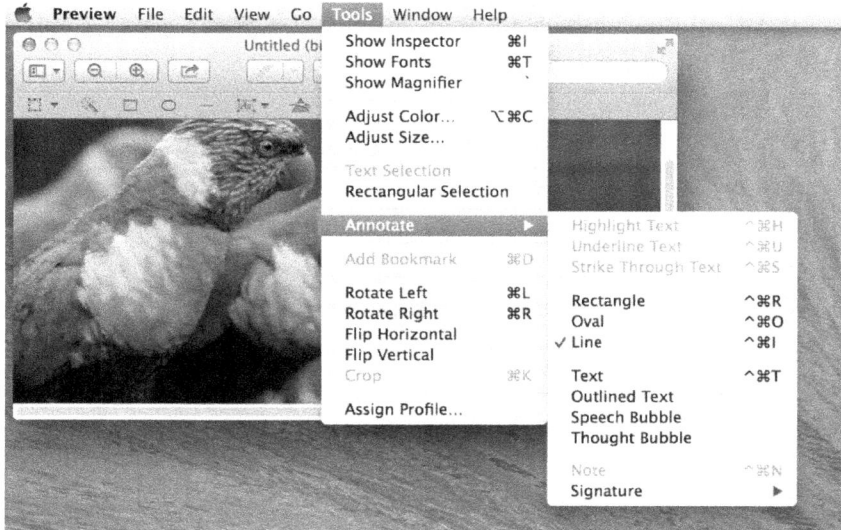

Here we have added an oval around one of the birds:

In fact I opened this screenshot in Preview and annotated with arrows and text. You can then export your annotated image.

You can use Preview to also view PDF files and edit them, and add annotations.

Be sure to make a duplicate of any file you open with Preview, so that the original does not get overwritten unintentionally.

# Chapter 30 – Mac OSX for Windows Users

Some of the information in this chapter will be repetitive, but it's a quick start guide for experienced Windows users switching to the Mac.

## Right Click

Unlike Windows, a Mac computer doesn't technically have a right click. However the Mac still has a method of clicking to bring up a popup menu like you are used to on Windows. The way to do it is to press the *control* key and then click your mouse or trackpad.
If you are using a trackpad instead of a mouse, and easy way to "right click" is to click using two fingers. This will bring up the pop up menu in the same way that control + click does.

You can also set up your trackpad to work in a more traditional Windows way. Use the following steps:

Click the Apple logo in the upper left corner of the menu bar:

Select System Preferences:

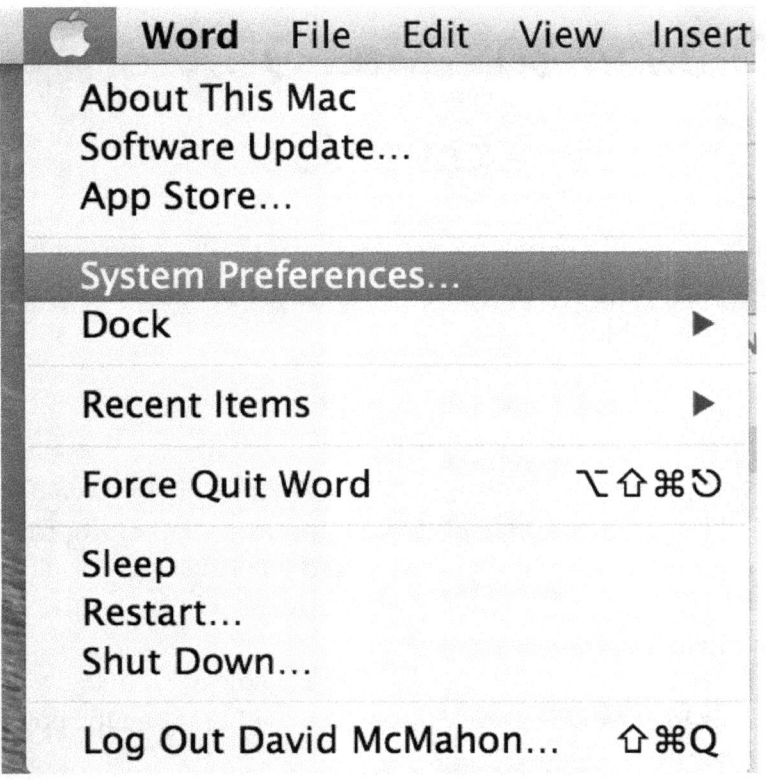

Go to the Hardware category and click on *Trackpad*. Now turn your attention to *Secondary Click*. By default, this is set to clicking with two fingers. To set up for a traditional Windows style right click, click open the drop down list:

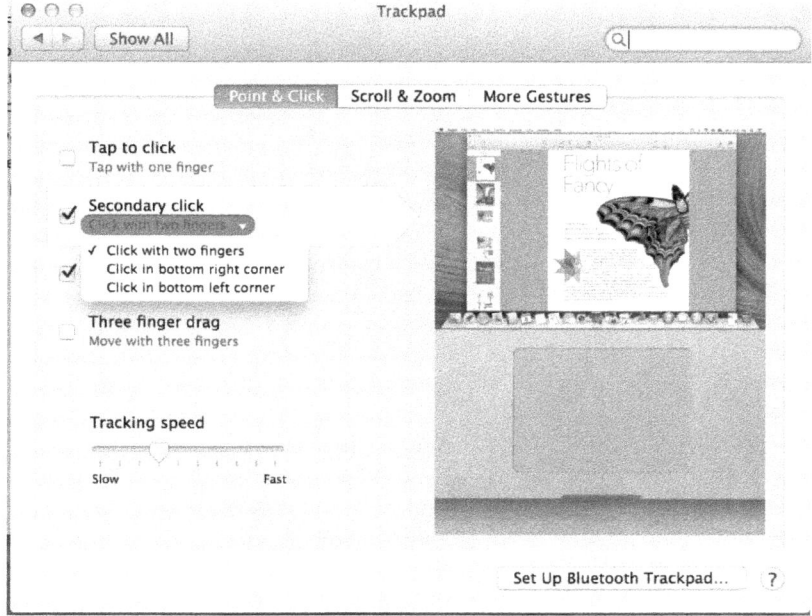

Select *Click in bottom right corner*. When you do this your trackpad will work like a trackpad on a Windows laptop, a left corner click will be the regular left mouse click and the right corner click will bring up the popup menu.

If using a Mouse, select *Mouse* from the System Preferences window and make sure secondary button is selected for the right mouse button:

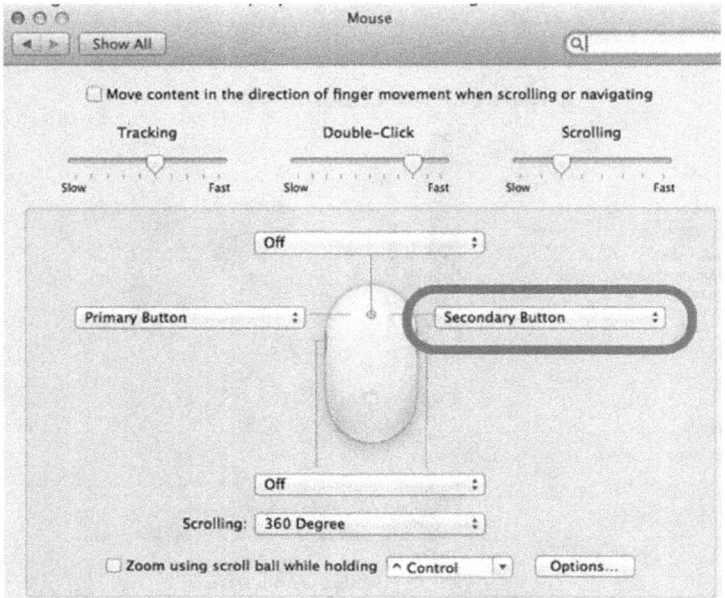

# Keyboard Shortcuts

Let's review again keyboard shortcuts on the Mac. First the symbols used on the Mac you should be familiar with.
**Command Key**

⌘ Command

The Command key is used extensively in Mac shortcuts. Be aware that when reading instruction materials or browsing menus the command key is indicated with the ⌘ symbol.

**Control Key**

^ Control

For beginning users the most important thing about the control key is right clicking. As noted here, the symbol for the control key is the carat.

### Option

⌥ Option

The option key resides in between your control and command keys on the left side of the spacebar. The symbol for the option key used in menus is this bizarre image ⌥

### Shift

The shift key is denoted on menus with ⇧.

### Tab

### Eject

To eject a disk or USB device, click the ⏏ symbol.


## Some Typical Commands

Now that we've reviewed the keyboard symbols, here are some typical keyboard and other commands.

**Undo:** ⌘Z

**Redo:** ⇧⌘Z

**Right Click:** ^click

**Windows control Key:** Not a strict analogy, but think of the command key (⌘) as doing much of the work of the Windows control key.

**Bring up display of open applications to switch to a new application:** ⌘+ ➜| (command +tab)

**Switch between open tabs in browser:** ⌃ + tab- tab (press control key and tab twice in quick succession with your web browser open)

**Force Quit:** ⌘+⌥+ESC (works like Ctrl-Alt-Delete in Windows)

**Hide Application:** ⌘+H (Hides an application from view, hiding all windows. To bring it back to the front, click the icon on the toolbar)

**Minimize Window:** ⌘+M (hides the currently active window, but will leave other windows from that application open).

**Delete vs. Backspace:** The *delete* key on a Mac works like a backspace key on a Windows PC. To use it like a PC delete key, press fn+delete

**Enter Key to Launch Application or Open File:** Pressing the enter key on a Mac will give you the option to rename a file. To open a file on a Mac, instead of pressing Enter double click with your mouse or trackpad.

**Application Properties:** Click on the application name in the menu bar, and select *Preferences*.

**Note on Closing windows:** Closing all open windows for an application will not shut down the application – it remains running. Either use the menu of the application to quit or press ⌘+Q

**The Taskbar**

Strictly speaking, there is not a taskbar on the Mac. However the dock functions in a relatively similar way, providing you with quick access to frequently used applications and folders by clicking on icons. The dock is by default found at the bottom of your screen.

**Corresponding Applications**

A Windows PC comes with a few built in applications like internet Explorer. Here we list the equivalent applications on a Mac.

**Notepad:** The equivalent application on a Mac is *Text Edit.* Note that Text Edit has rich text editing features so is also equivalent to word pad.

**Internet Explorer:** To browse the web on a Mac, the default option is *Safari*. The Safari icon can be found on your dock:

You can also download third party web browsers like Google Chrome.

## System Configuration

For system configuration, use the System Preferences window. It can be opened by clicking the icon:

Found on your dock or in the applications folder of Finder.

www.ingramcontent.com/pod-product-compliance
Lightning Source LLC
Chambersburg PA
CBHW071214050326
40689CB00011B/2325